CANCER
Determination and Me

ARNIE HIGGS

authorHOUSE®

AuthorHouse™ UK
1663 Liberty Drive
Bloomington, IN 47403 USA
www.authorhouse.co.uk
Phone: 0800.197.4150

Published by AuthorHouse 02/05/2015

ISBN: 978-1-4969-9951-1 (sc)
ISBN: 978-1-4969-9950-4 (hc)
ISBN: 978-1-4969-9952-8 (e)

Contents

CANCER
Determination and Me

motivation
inspires
others
x

This book is to a great friend Chris Rayner 1995-2014

But dedicated to my mum x

When I was diagnosed, I thought to myself my new path in life is to become a social worker/ motivator for patients and families that have suffered from cancer. I didn't get the grades to do so but I thought of ways to not give up because I was so determined to help so I thought if I don't achieve the qualification to go into a hospital and sit face to face with a patient, I will send in books to help. This is one of my books which I want help someone.

If I can just make one person smile, that will make my day. x

My life and my perspective on life have changed dramatically since I was diagnosed with a brain tumor in August 2008. I have missed a lot of school and study time because of the intense and lengthy treatment I have received. I have had to Re-learn basic skills, especially basic physical skills that most people take for granted, such as writing, walking and other every day activities. I believe that this experience has made me a more determined and a motivated person. I have had to work very hard to get my life back but I have never complained or given in. The words that got me though everything where 'No pain no gain' I will look forward to using my inner strength as I go forward in life.

You think to yourself it will never happen to me, but it does and it did, being diagnosed with cancer changed everything and the fact that I never lost one friend but gained more, so many people were there to support me and me knowing I had friends that cared so much for me just gave me even more courage to beat cancer and I did. I used to be an all round sports man, play all different sorts of sport from being captain of the cross country running team to goal keeper of football and any other sport that interested me. I used to be so motivated in running and playing my sports but one day my life changed, it was like the lights just went out and I had to stop every physical activity I loved to do and did every day of my life.

Acknowledgements

Firstly I would like to say my thank you's.

- The first thanks goes to my mummy for being there 24/7, helping me up the hospital in so many different ways as possible doing anything I asked her to do, for loving me and taking the time to understand my needs and the generosity of giving up her life to help me and support me. I love you mum

- The second thanks goes to my dad for motivating me, getting me to my local sports centre swimming, to the gym and generally keeping me going, making me laugh, keeping me happy and doing normal things - his attitude was " no pain no gain " love you pappa

- Third To my sister Sherry; I just want to give you a big thank you and a huge hug for having the patience of a saint in taking your time and effort in treating me as normally as possible but also taking into consideration that I was not well, looking after me as much as possible. I love you so much bells

- And to the best brother Billy I love you mate thank you for coming back from Afghan and looking after me. You were there for the whole 6 weeks of terror supporting me and I know it was hard for you to see me not eating properly but I'm better now, I love you

- A massive thank you to my Auntie Margaret and my Uncle Ian for being there for me and keeping my mum occupied and for looking after my mum whilst my brother and I were at the hospital, 5 days a week for 6 weeks I love you sooo much

- Thank you to Chay Mafia and the Mafia family you are a great mate always got time for me and you looked after me I love you mate, The song you dedicated to me (Bill Withers - Lean On Me)

- To Thomas O'Connell and the O'Connell family Charlie Flanery and the Flanery family, Josh Dean and the Dean family to Rob Smith and the Smith family, Sibel Aslim and to Kerry Heywood they have all shown their true colours and what wonderful people you are, so much generosity, calmness and friendship. I love you all

- And a big thank you to Tommy Archer and the Archer family, Tommy Ryan and the Ryan family. Harry Edgar and the Edgar family, Bayden Brown, Tarsi Tigere, Lewis Sciota and the Sciota family and all the people I have met on the way though my recovery I just want to thank you all for just being there and treating me as normally as possible but remembering that I struggled with my physical activities.

- A massive thank you to Reshma Patel at Templeman Opticians for spotting the tumour – you saved my life you are an angel in disguise, all my love and thanks.

- Big thank you to Jack Chester a top man who motivated me when I felt down, your always in my mind mate, never forgotten. 1991-2010 R.I.P.

- Chris rayner top top man I love you so much mate this book is for you mate, never forgoten, 1995-2014

- Just want to say a main thank you to Chay Mafia, Tommy Archer, Tommy Ryan, Tom O'Connell, Bayden Brown, Harry Edgar, Tarsi Tigere your the main boys, yes yes, Love you all boys

- Thanks to my cousins Jack Gaunt, Bobby Gaunt, Sam Gaunt, Tommy Gaunt and Gary Steeves cheers lads.

- My brother Christphor Higgs you was always cruel to be kind but I know you always meent well and you love me to bits.

- Thank you to Dr Curnock, Mr. Norris, Mr. Wilson, Mr. Gurlin, Mr. Foot and all at De La Salle School and Langue's college for taking the time to understand what I went through and supporting my needs, I really appreciate your support.

- A great big thank you to Teens Unite for being so kind and giving me great support we all had some great days out and Christmas parties - you are all wonderfull and loving people that cares for every single one of us.

- TEENAGE CANCER TRUST I want to thank you ever so much for the biggest support ever, the great surprises and the awesome days out. It is people like you that put a smile on people's faces by just supporting everyone, spreading your love, care and fantastic positive attitude towards life.

- To all the nures at Basildon hosptial wagtail ward my local you was great love yas all.

- To my big sisters Joanne Higgs, I remember coming round and you giving me big bear hugs and looked after me when I was with you. I love ya. Your little bro, Arn x

- To all the girls at the Pavillion cafe in Southend Karen Khemiri, Karen Kinnish thank you for not treating me like a ill person great support and loving people thank you Karen Khemiri " wink wink"

- To Anne Watters for helping me to write this fantastic book.

Introduction

Hello my name is Arnie Higgs and I was living a normal 13 year old teenager's life, playing football, having a laugh with my mates and just generally mucking about living life at its full when for some unknown reason I started to get serious headaches which I can only describe as really bad brain freeze and morning sickness. Being an all round sports man, captain of cross country team vice captain of my school rugby team goal keeper for my school team and Sunday league the last thing on my mind was cancer. I was a keen runner, I ran for an hour every morning, got home had a shower, a bit of breakfast then bike to school to attend befor school sports.

I started to be sick every morning and I was having bad headaches. My mum thought I was doing too much exercise and I was not eating and sleeping properly. My Mum and I automatically thought I was over working myself. We went to my local GP 3 times in a case of 3 monts they looked in my eyes, took my temperature, height, weight etc. They didn't see anything wrong with me, and then they started to ask questions then said "are you sad" "are you being bullied" and I said "No I am a happy go lucky lad that has a laugh and joke loving life" the doctor diagnosed me with anxiety my mum and I were curious and confused because I didn't have anything to worry about, we just left the GP thinking it will go in a couple of days but a month went by and I was still getting these headaches and morning sickness, we went back to the GP and they did exactly the same thing as last time height, weight and etc and they asked me the same questions and I said "no I'm fine I'm just getting really bad headaches and sickness", they still said I had anxiety so once again my mum and I didn't think anything of it and went home happily.

A month went by and I was struggling, so my mum made an appointment at the GP and they did exactly the same as the last times, by this time my mum was not very happy because I was not getting any better. So the next day my mum made an appointment at my local optician thinking it might be migraine they said "ok we will fit you in for tomorrow".

Tomorrow came and I was out with my mates, we went back to my house then Charlie Flanery, Rob Smith and I rode our bikes down there, my Mum following slowly behind with Buster our dog. Then Mum and I went into the opticians and when the lady was looking in my eyes I noticed that she was looking in my left eye the most. I got the feeling that she was getting worried when she noticed something behind my left eye that was not supposed to be there. The optician ran out the room leaving me in the seat while she was talking to my Mum, then at the click of a finger she was on the phone to my local GP asking them to have a look in my left eye because she could see pressure behind it so we went to my GP, which luckily is a 2 minute walk.

My doctor looked in my left eye and said it must be very small because I can't see anything, so there's my Mum and I confused, we went back to my optician and we said they can't see anything so the optician phoned Southend Eye Hospital TELLING them that I needed an MRI scan as soon as possible. By this time my mum was getting worried; I didn't really know what was going on I just thought I had migraine, so I left my Mum and rode off on my bike with my friends we were going to go back to their house, but on the way I was thinking. I said "I'm going home to see my Mum so goodbye see yous tomorrow". Before I knew it, it was late and I had to go to bed because I had to go to Southend Eye Hospital the next morning.

From This day, This is where my journy starts though cancer.

I WANT TO INSPIRE PEOPLE. I WANT SOMEONE TO LOOK AT ME AND SAY "BECAUSE OF YOU, I DIDN'T GIVE UP."

Chapter One

EARLY CHILDHOOD

Late one afternoon in May, 1995, I Arnie Victor Higgs was born and arrived at Basildon Hospital kicking and screaming my head off like usual, getting taking away from my Mum straightaway because I had the umbilical cord wrapped around my neck making me more agitated. I was finally given me back to my Mum, who gave me a big kiss on the head and the best cuddle you could think of, and since then I have been a happy child.

Coming home from the hospital to a wonderful house, toys, balloons and banners everywhere made me feel loved when I was about two I got my first Arsenal shirt; I was jumping up and down like a yo yo.

Started to go to play school, having a fun time running about like a headless chicken loving it, making towers out of wooden blocks, having milk and biscuits, making biscuits and then eating them, and as I always try to do chatting up a couple of girls like always put a cheeky smile on my face.

Finally going into nursery had a couple of tumbles in there tripping up and fell on the corner of a wooden toy box and splitting the top of my head open did not make me very happy but other days in nursery were fun finger painting, playing in the sandpit, riding on the tricycles had the best time ever but one day silly me I did not know what a pencil sharpener was so I put my finger in and turned it; blow me I screamed at the top of my voice my mum and Dad came to pick me up my dad said to me I bet that hurt but you have taught your self there son but loving as my Dad is he still made me laugh and my mum dad and I went home on the way my mum bought me a big ice cream to make me happy.

Going into Infants School made me feel a big boy learning how to read and write. I had my first Sports Day. I ran the 90 metre sprint race, the 200 metre race and the hurdles. I won all the races and I remember like it was yesterday my Mum saying if you get three 1st place stickers you can put them as eyes and a nose and draw a smiley mouth on your t-shirt. I still remember when I was in year 5 I won everything and the words that came out my teachers mouth were "Arnie can you lose this race because the children are getting jealous so I said ok, when we were at the starting line for 50 metre hurdles and my mate next to me said Arnie let me win please and I said ok mate. The teacher said on your marks, get set, GO! and I ran like the wind blows, jumping over these hurdles like a horse and I won the race. My Mum told me afterwards that most of the boys did not even jump the hurdles, but ran past them to try to beat me.

At the end of year 5 I started to play football with my mates at lunch time I used to bring in my goalie gloves and my Arsenal goal keepers shirt and play in goal even playing it every morning. This one night my family and I went to Lakeside shopping centre and my Mum and Dad bought me the new Arsenal home goal keepers top.

The next morning I went to school, showed everyone the shirt and everyone put it on so I put it back on and then we started to play. Within about 10 minutes of the game I ran out to get the ball and collided with my friend and I fell on the floor, putting all my body weight though my left arm I dinent feel anything. But I then looked down at my arm and saw that it was all bent with blood everywhere and I couldn't move my wrist. I guess I was too shocked to cry or scream so I got up and walked to the first aid room. As I walked though the door The lady shot up from her seat and helped me onto the bed and gave me a sick bowl and then she shouted to reception saying, "call an ambulance". The paramedics came and said to me we have to cut the sleeve of my goaley top and I heard my mum in the back ground saying "oh no we only bought that for arnie last night," laughing as she said "try pull his arm though the sleeve" but it was to bad so they had to cut my sleeve. I then hobbled onto an ambulance, my arm in a sling crying my eyes out because at this point I could see and feel what had happened. Getting rushed to Basildon Hospital in the back of an ambulance with blue flashing lights, sirens made me wheezy getting sent straight into A&E where I was seen straight away. An x-ray confirmed I had snapped my Radius bone and my Ulna bone in my lower arm. This meant I had to have an operation to insert metal plates.

Two weeks went by and I was back at school playing football, my mate said to me I'm a better goal keeper then you Arnie so I said "let's have a penalty shoot out" so we did 5 shoots each. I saved 4 and he saved 2 and I said look "I even beat you with a broken arm if my mum had found out about me let alone playing football but being in goal she would have had a go at me only because she cared but before I knew it my teachers had grassed me up and told her already haha.

I went home and my Mum had a go at me for going in goal but I was proud of myself because I was the best goalkeeper in my primary school. I got picked to play for the school football team, I was only young at the time but I was good and we won, lost and drew games but mostly won, our last game in year 6 we won 3-1 at the end of the game a man came up to me and said you are really good, "do you fancy playing in goal for my under 12s Sunday league football team (Copeland colts F.C)" so I said "yeah definitely."

Chapter Two

YOUNG BOY, BECOMING A TEENAGER

Becoming a teenager made me feel more important, taking over the role and becoming "man of the house" because my Mum and Dad split up when I was 11 due to my mum drinking alcohol, I didn't let it upset me, well it didn't really upset me because I didn't really clock on what was wrong with it but my dad just didn't like it so he left, but I just carried on with my normal happy life playing football and having a laugh with my friends, whilst in the middle of joining a big new secondary school called De la Salle.

I was a chirpy little lad, happy go lucky and on the first day of secondary school I was going around meeting everyone talking to them and just meeting new friends. Because I was a nice person I made a few friends straightaway, sitting next to each other in class and playing football with them, that day we had P.E (physical education) lesson and it was athletics. We started off warming up talking to each other then we had to run 400 metres around the track. At that age I didn't really know what a 400 metre run was so when the teacher blew the whistle I just ran as fast as I could all the way round the track and a quarter of the way around the track I was out of breath and had a stitch but I was well in front but because I was determined to win everything I didn't stop and just kept running. I must have stayed at least 30 metres in front of everyone else. From then on I made more friends because I was good at PE.

I remember going home that night and bumping in to some boys on their bikes near my house and I heard them say to each other "that's that really fast kid that goes to our school "and I was like "allo boys you alright nice to meet you" I started hanging out with them, I found out it was Bayden Brown, Owen Hillum Jake Ellis and Tarsi Tigere getting the train to school with them and I made really good friends with them as they lived so close to me. We were going out on our bikes, going around each other's houses and having a laugh everyday.

About 2 weeks went by and I noticed a sign on the wall in the PE department saying "football try outs on Tuesday "so I thought I'll have some of that.

When we were all getting ready in the changing room raring to go, I slipped my England yellow goal keepers shirt on which at the time I loved Sponge Bob so I got the name Sponge Bob 1 on the back of my shirt which made every one laugh. We all went out on the field to play football and we had a good game. The next day I saw on the Notice Board in the PE department "De la Salle Year 7 football team fixtures" and I was on there as number one goal keeper, a big smile was on my face. From then things were going well everyone started to call me Sponge Bob I turned into the class clown making a laugh of everything, being naughty, talking back to teachers and everyone just loved me.

There was one time I was in class and I had a Catherine Tate voice remote and that lesson I wasn't doing my work, I was talking to my mates eating in class and my teacher shouted across the room " Arnie go stand outside ". I said "no" and he then said "I will report you to the Headmaster and get you sent to detention". The room went quiet and I had my little Catherine Tate voice tape in my hand under the table and I pressed the button and it said "am I bothered,", does my face seem "bothered", "i ain't bothered tho"" and everyone was just laughing and rolling on the floor. There was other times I used to get up in front of class and start singing and doing voice over's from funny programs, I used to do a bit of stand up comedy as well everyone loved me. I even remember when we had a substitue teacher in and I was eating in class and the teacher told me off and said put them in the bin and I piped up and said I can't miss - these are my diabetic crisps but I wasent evan diabetic.

I have had times where I have had fights in school, there was this one time where I went out with this girl, but it was my mates girlfriend. They were going out and one day I kissed her without him knowing and he got the hump with me, later that day when we had PE and we were playing 2 aside football in the sports hall. Me and my mate, Chay Mafia, were the best in the class and we were beating everyone and the next game was against the boy that had the hump with me. We were running around and he went to kick me so I got out of the way and tripped him up and I laughed at him and I just carried on playing and I see him running up behind me and then he rugby tackled me to the floor, holding my hands so I just started pushing him away with my feet and kicking him a couple of times and dragged him up by his top and pushed him down to the floor. Then my teacher dragged me off him and sent me to my Head teacher and I was excluded for two weeks.

I had my ups and downs, laughs and jokes in year 7 and 8. At that age I used to just take the piss and muck about, but I still concentrated on school work and my football! Outside of school I was just playing football with my Sunday league team and what not and just doing what a young boy did in his spare time. Year 7 went by really quick and along came year 8 and I started different lessons, achieving different grades but still my happy self I started to get closer to my sports like running, rugby basketball and athletics.

I spent most of my free time in the PE department and when I was not playing football with my mates I became a part of the rugby team, basketball team and the running team. I then became Vice Captain of the rugby team, Captain of the running team, number 1 goalkeeper of the football team and played for the school basketball team.

I represented De La Salle School in many different sports and won and lost. I remember when the class had to run to Gloucester Park and run round the pond around I used to run around the pond seven times and and most of the class ran round three times but I still made it back before the others. Lately I started to get really bad headaches which I could only describe as "brain freeze" and I was being sick every morning. One time when I was out with my mates sometimes I just had to get on the floor and curl into ball and hold my head because the headaches hurt that much one time this person walked passed and said to my friends "is he all right?" and my mates just said "yes he just got brain freeze." My Mum thought I was doing too much exercise and maybe I was not eating and sleeping properly, my Mum and I just automatically thought I was overworking myself, but I guess not.

Chapter Three

GETTING TOLD THE BAD NEWS

The headaches were happening frequently and I was being sickness every morning when I woke up but I just carried on with my normal life, weeks went by and I couldn't stand it anymore so my Mum made and appointment to see my doctor at my local GP. The date came and we went to my local GP who looked into my eyes, he took my temperature, height, weight and etc. He didn't see anything wrong with me, Then started to ask questions "are you sad" "are you being bullied" and I said "No I am a happy go lucky lad that has a laugh and joke whilst loving life" the doctor did not have anything else to say so he just diagnosed me with anxiety.

So My Mum and I were curious and confused because I didn't have anything to worry about. We just left the GP thinking it will go in a couple of days so I was just going to school as usual playing football, being the class clown but these headaches were still happening. The headaches were just like the wind, they would just come and go unexpected but a month went by and the headaches and morning sickness were just getting worse. I started to stay in bed longer, I had no energy so my Mum and I went back to the GP, the doctor did exactly the same as last time, he took my height and weight and etc. They asked me the same questions and I said "no I'm fine I'm just getting really bad headaches and sickness", they still said I had anxiety so once again my Mum and I didn't think anything of it and went home.

A month went by and I was still doing what I normally do playing football for my Sunday league team, going football training, going to school and playing out with my friends but I was really struggling but (I never showed it to anyone except my mum), so my Mum made another appointment at the GP and they did exactly the same as the last times. By this time my Mum was not happy because I was not getting any better truth be told I was getting worse so my mum raised her voice a bit and said "what on earth is going on heare you are a profesional dr and you keep saying my boy has anxiaty he clearley hasent so do somthing about it please" the next day my mum made an appointment at my local optician thinking it might be migraine they said "ok we will fit you in for tomorrow".

Tomorrow came and I was out with my mates out on our bikes riding around. Then we rode back to my house and we only had 5 minutes to get there for my appointment so my Mum just said you ride up there and I'll catch up with you behind. So me, Charlie, Rob, and Josh rode our bikes down there, my mum following slowly behind with Buster our dog.

I went into the opticians my mates waited outside and the lady said where is your Mum. I said she's on her way and the lady said I can't see you without your mum because you are underage so I thought fair enough and I sat down and my Mum walked in. Mum and I then went into the optician's room where the lady was looking in my eyes. I noticed that she was looking in my left eye the most, and I got the feeling that she was getting worried, when she noticed something behind my left eye that was not supposed to be there. The optician ran out the room, leaving me in the seat, she was talking to my mum, then at the click of a finger she was on the phone to my local GP asking them to have a look in my left eye because she could see pressure behind it so we went to my GP, which luckily is a 1 minute walk up the road so my doctor looked in my left eye and said it must be very small because he couldn't see anything. Then me and my Mum were confused, so we went back to my optician and told the optician that the doctor said they couldn't see anything so the optician phoned Southend eye hospital TELLING them that I needed an MRI scan as soon as possible. By this time my mum was getting worried, I didn't really know what was going on because I was still with my mates not really concentrating on what was happening I just thought I had migraine, so I left my mum and I rode off on my bike with my friends. We were going to go back to their house but on the way I was thinking, so I said "I'm going home now boys to see my mum so I will see you all tomorrow". When I got home, my Mum was sitting there with a worried look on her face before I knew it, it was late and I had to go to bed because I had to go to Southend Eye Hospital the next morning.

It was about 6 o'clock the next morning when I woke up and just laid there thinking what is the matter? All kinds of thoughts were going through my mind but cancer was not one of them, my Mum walked into my room telling me to get ready because Auntie Margaret is picking us up in half an hour to take us to the hospital so I just got up, got dressed went downstairs where my Mum and Auntie were sitting in the living room having a coffee so I said "come on then, let's go, so we all got in the car drove to Southend Eye Hospital where we waited for about 2 hours. They finally called me in and they put some orange dye in my eyes and told me to have a seat because it takes 10 minutes for that stuff to work. So in the ten minutes we were sitting there having a cup of tea, reading a magazine keeping our eyes on the clock. By this time, it was 11 o 'clock and we were seen. They looked into my eyes, saw the pressure so they sent me for a MRI scan ASAP the same day.

On the way to the MRI department we stopped to have a bite to eat in the hospital café and when we had finished our brunch we made our way to the MRI department. When we got there they told me to take off my clothes and put a hospital gown on. Then I lay on the bed and they started putting this neck strap on me and strapping me down. I was getting wary and I didn't know what was happening then it started all these loud noises. Half way through the MRI, I was injected with some dye this is to make the organs stand out so you can see them better but as soon as they injected me with the dye I started to feel sick and because I had all the neck straps on I couldn't get up so I started pressing the pannic button and I was moving about because I felt like I wanted to be sick so they said are you sure you want to be sick and I said yes then they asked my again " are you sure" I said " yes I do now hurry up" so they started to take the neck brace off and I shot up and I was sick all over the floor. I was sick because the dye reacted with the tumour. They did'nt say that but that is what I think because when I finished and was in remission I had loads of mri scans and when they inserted the dye I was fine and still am till this day.

We still didn't know what was wrong but then we had to go see a doctor in the ocean ward for children when my Auntie, Mum and I went into the ward we were waiting in the waiting area to see the doctor on the ward we was waiting like 2 hours. When he came a nurse took me away to play on the computers with her whilst my Auntie and my Mum were in the room with the doctor. This is when the doctor told my mum I had the brain tumour the size of an apricot, which now I think is terrible on a trained doctors behalf because you go to a doctor with all your trust, prepared to hear the correct news but for mis- diagnosing me with such a big thing makes me mad and to know that when we finally found out what it was my sister aged 14, still in school, looked on Google for symptoms of headaches and sickness and the first thing that came up was brain tumour, brain tumour, brain tumour. So if a 14 year old girl can find that out and a trained doctor misses it, that is terrible. Through my travels of this cancer story I have heard so many of the same stories of mis- diagnosis told to me. But anyway back to the book I went to my bed and had a bit of dinner I still dont know what is the matter, I saw my Mum walk down the hall as if she had seen a ghost or as if she was a ghost I had finished my dinner and I got into bed. My Mum slept in a bed beside me and we both watched TV and films. The nurses were on the phone all night getting in contact with St Georges Hospital, Kings Cross Hospital and Great Ormond Street Hospital to see who had a bed first because It was urgent. The first hospital was St Georges in Tooting, London so the next morning my mum and I had an ambulance waiting for us, from Southend hospital.

All the way to St Georges Hospital in London we had blue flashing lights and sirens whilst going up there and I loved it because well I didn't know or realize what was going on or I kind of knew but didn't know it was cancer or a tumour or even if it was a really critical, deathly illness well I didn't know what was wrong with me. I was just sitting there smiling and on my phone and looking in a magazine and it said there was a new film coming out in three days from now so I rang my mate Charlie Flannery up and said do you want to go and see this new film on Wednesday and he said yes, go for it me thinking that there is nothing wrong with me and I'll be home the next day. Then we arrived at the hospital where they welcomed me into the ward. I remember waiting quite a while for a bed because it was quite busy, I feelings I got was horibel because it was a oldish hosptial and it was realy warm and dull in there it was dark outside and I just didn't feel comfortable. It must have been visiting time because there were lots of people around. But eventually I was given a bed in the corner of the ward. I got myself sorted out into my bed and that and about half hour later the surgeon come to my bed and said follow me into my office so I went with my Mum and my Aunt and the doctor explained to me what a brain tumour was and what they would have to do to remove it. As I was only 13 years of age, I did not know what cancer was, I was calling it a tumour but I didn't know what it was; I just piped up and said "right come on then, let's get it over and done with".

I was then told about the risks of the operation and once again I did not know what it was all about so I didn't really listen – however, my Mum and my Aunt were listening. My Mum then explained what the consequences would be and what could happen. Then I just said "let's do it". Due to the fact that I was only 13 years of age, my Mum had to give her consent for the operation. That night back on the Ward, we were sitting there watching television and then I fell asleep, I guess I dread to thing what was going though my mums head, The night before I went down for my operation, I remember seeing a young boy, who had just been brought in who looked "like a zombie" from his operation He slept and slept and he had a drain hanging from his head which was filled with blood. This really frightened me, so I said to my Mum "will this happen to me?". She told me not to be silly and everything will be all right.

The next day I woke up, it was the morning and I went down for my operation. This was the operation to remove the fluid that was building pressure in the back of the head. A hole had to be drilled in the front of my skull and a tube was inserted to drain off the excess fluid that had built up. This made it easier for the major operation for the removal of the tumour.

I remember waking up from the operation when they brought me back around and I remember sitting up with a smile on my face and thanking the doctor and I shook his hand because I thought that was the major operation to remove the tumour, but of course this was only the operation to insert the tube. For the next six days, I had to stay in bed because the drip only worked on gravity, i.e. the tube had to be level with my shoulders at all times I was only allowed to get up for five minutes at a time so that I could go to the toilet!

Thanks to my mates, Charlie and Josh, who came to visit me during those six days of complete boredom, which really cheered me up, as I was allowed to get out of bed and sit on the chair, but when I was in the chair the tube still had to be adjusted so that it was at the same height of gravity, but that didn't bother me much as my mates were there to take my mind off it.

The day before my major operation, I was lying there alone, my mum was in the kitchen, just making a cup of tea and something to eat then somthing amazing happened.....I thought I was dreaming when I saw this big man in a sandy, camouflage outfit walk down to my bed. Surprisingly enough this was my older brother Bill who is in the British Army and at the time serving out in Afghanistan in Camp Bastion. He had got flown back as soon as he heard that I was not well.

My Brother Bill

I was very pleased to see my brother Bill and when he came to the bedside the first thing he did was to give me a big hug and a kiss he said "alright mate i'm here now".

As I did not get to see him very much due to him being in the Army, the big hug bill gave me it give me a magical, breathless feeling.

Bill gave me his "dog tag and his ID cards and told me to look after these and I would be all right". So I slept with them that night under my pillow. I did not get a very good sleep that night due to the major operation the next day and the uncomfortableness of the tube in the side of my head.

"This is the start of where my life get's tipped upside down."

Monday morning came and I had to miss breakfast and I was laying there in bed and the operating trolley came down the ward. They told me to get on it, so I stood up and clenched my hands tight holding my brother's ID cards and "dog tag".

I do not remember feeling nervous because I did not know what to expect. As we came into the pre-operation room, everyone was lovely, friendly and they told me what they were going to do so they took my temperature and put the oxygen mask over my face. It was a strange feeling, but I liked it because I felt relaxed and like I was just dropping into a deep sleep, I was trying to play a game to see how long I could keep my eyes open for and not let them shut and before I knew it, I was "sparko"

During the operation, believe it or not, I could see myself having the operation. It was as if I was floating above and looking down on myself being operated on I believe that, that had something to do with my angels coming down and helping me realize what was going on. 10 hours went by, they tried to wake me up but apparently from what my brother told me he was walking back from the shop in hospital and he was just round the corner and he heard someone screaming and shouting and "F'ing and blinding" so he ran around the corner and it was me. So he went up to the bed and he was talking to the doctors asking them if I was all right and they told him it was just the anaesthetic wearing off, and that they would be taking me to the Intensive Care Unit just so that I could recover a bit.

The first thing I could remember coming back from my surgery was that I was laying in a hospital bed I dident know what the time was but I just thought it was the morning so I opend my eyes and see that I was in hosptial but I said im going to jump out this bed run up to the ward and see everyone and open all my get well cards and have some sweets and that but then I said to my self ill just have another hour in bed and befor I knew it I opend my eyes and the first thing I saw was my sister looking through the metal bars of the hosptial bed. The first thing I said to her was in my crackley pasty voice "you alright, gay". And She just laughed!

We just had a general chat, then I remember feeling a terrible pain in my penis so I told my sister to get bill our brother. I said to bill, "cor bill my willy really hurts" he said it was the catheter. I was constantly tugging at this to try and get it off and he told me not to pull this out. I remember thinking that the nurses in the ICU were playing about with the bed because it felt like I was on a blow up bed and they kept letting it down and pumping it back up. So I said to my brother go tell them to stop it because it was annoying me. I had a very uncomfortable afternoon, but all my family were at my bedside.

I had a very uncomfortable sleep during the night and at one point, I was sick all over myself and my bed and it was so annoying at the time because the nurses had to come and clean it up. She was moving me from left to right, wiping the bed and wiping my body which was so annoying because I was feeling so tired and in agony. Eventually I went back to sleep and I remember waking up about 7 o'clock as I didn't know what the time was but it felt like 7 o'clock in the morning I was the next morning the nurses dropped me off back at the ward. I was very uncomfortable and felt like I had to go the toilet. I was really busting and I said to someone I wanted to go to the toilet so they gave me one of those cardboard things to have a wee in bed. I did not know what it was, but I just could not go to the toilet in one of those things. I was really bursting to go a wee and was not allowed to get up but I thought "sod It, so I made myself get up out of bed. I finally got up and I felt like an old man that was wobbling and I couldn't see properly and felt wobbly and dizzy. I had everyone behind me saying I was not allowed to get up and they were all saying get back down I remember hearing my mum behind the hospital curtains crying, which I think is really sad but here we have it as old Frank Sinatra says "that's life" well I still managed to get up. I eventually then used a commode that was next to my bed. When I got up to go to the toilet on the commode, I could not see out of my left eye and I was all over the place, wobbly everyone was holding me and had their arm on me. I just assumed that the sight in this eye would return in a couple of minutes and my balance would come back. I filled the commode up with about 3 litres of urine and was told I should not keep that much fluid inside me.

Through the day I started to feel a bit awake and they let me free of ALL the tubes wires that was attached to me and about 6 o'clock that evening I got on my feet and I felt free from the wires and tubes but felt strange that I did not have any balance and could not use my left arm. I thought maybe this was something which would come back tomorrow. Then I started to walk to the bed opposite me just for a bit of exercise and to get the blood running and moving about and then I noticed that I could not walk properly.

I was not afraid or scared about the way I was walking because I thought it was just general laziness as I had just come out of the operation and been asleep for a while, so I sat down and had a bit of dinner and I noticed that I could not use my left hand properly with my knife and fork which was a bit strange and frustrating. So I was just eating with my hands. It got later and later and everyone had all gone and it was just me and my mum we was laying there together watching tv. It was nice, she kept saying do you want anything to eat or drink and I just said no thank you and before I knew it I was asleep So I went to sleep that night and it was an uncomfortable sleep but probably one of the most comfortable sleeps I had had for a couple of weeks because I had stitches in the top of my head and staples in the back of my head which was all plastered up and soft to lay on and I was free from all the wires. I woke up in the morning and I was really hungry this was about 5 in the morning I turned over and tapped my mum on the head as she was still asleep and said can you do me some breakfast please mummy so she got up and about five minutes later she came back and said, Arn do you know what the time is haha she said it was 4:55 and the ward kitchen for patients was closed so we just went back to sleep.

I the woke up about 8:30 and just put my bed side tv on and it said " tv don't come on till 9 o' clock " so I just listened to the radio. It was 9 o'clock and I woke my mum up and asked her if she can do me some breakfast so I had a bowl of cereal then when I finished that I said mum I still feel hungry can you do me some more please so she did and I ate that bowl finished it and said mum I'm still hungry can you do me some toast and a cup of tea please so she looked at me and said ok my little big man, I must admit that was the best slice of toast and cup of tea in the world it went down a treat My Mum's phone rang and it was my Aunt and she said she was just coming up in the lift and she said "I want to see Arnie walk to the lift and meet me there". So I thought to myself "yes, I am going to walk I am going to do it". So I walked from my bed to the start of the Ward but it was a struggle but I did it and walked to the lift, which was only 20/30 metres away but I had to hold on to my Mum's arm and in my right arm, another crutch.

I got to the lift, but I had to sit down because I was very tired and the doors opened and there was my Auntie. She raised her voice in a funny way at me and said "why are you in your wheelchair?" so my Mum said he did walk here but he had to sit down because he was tired. So she came running out of the lift and gave me a big cuddle and said "well done".

During the next three weeks, it was just the same old thing, lying in bed watching television. I felt closed in because I could not do anything on my own. Thank God for my brother Bill and sister Sherry coming up to see me as well as my cousins, Bobby, Jack, Sam, Tommy and Gary. I remember something really funny with my brother. I did not think this was funny, but my brother was "cracking up". Someone bought me a Get Well Soon balloon which was tied to the bottom of my bed. My brother used to sit at the bottom of the bed and he used to tap it to me and he said to me you have got to use your left arm to try and hit it back to me but because I could not see out of my left eye and had no co-ordination, I kept missing the balloon. My left arm was just floppy. It was a helium balloon and before I could tap it the balloon it had gone back up into the air they were all laughing. I did not know if they were "taking the mick" or they were just laughing because it was quite a good funny game. Obviously they told me they were not laughing at me they were laughing with me and I was cracking up because it was funny.

My Aunt came up and she bought me a brand new PSP – play station portable – I used to like those sort of things, but what was "gutting" was that I could not use it because I did not have any co-ordination in my left hand so it just sat there in its box at my bed side.

During the times when it was just me and my Mum, it was a bit quiet but if it was not for my Mum, I would not have been able to do anything because no matter what time it was when it was if I had asked my Mum for something, for example a bit of toast or a cup of tea, she would go and get it for me, or if I just had the urge for a packet of cheese and onion crisps, she would get up out of the bed that she was in next to mine and go to the shop and get if for me.

My Mum even had to help me to the bathroom and bath me which was a bit embarrassing as I was a 13 year old teenager. (This really annoyed me so because it was all there in my head, I knew what to do but was physically unable to do it). But all in all it was so nice just to spend that much time and be so close to my mum for six weeks was fantastic shame it had to be in that situation to get that feeling and from those days I am soooo, soooo, sooo close to my mummy I love her so much I love you mummzy.

During those difficult four weeks, my Mum was unbelievable, she was like an "angel" she would just jump when I said anything. She used to help me in many ways from getting me up and walking up and down the Ward. She put me in the wheelchair and took me downstairs to the cafeteria because it was just a different scenery. Sometimes we used to sit there and have something to eat together. Mum, I just want to thank you so much and I love you!

A couple of days later, we finally got "kicked out" of hospital and sent back home. I remember the car ride back from the hospital in my brother's Mercedes. My brother was not the tidiest of persons and his car was kind of full up with rubbish which did not help the space for all my hospital bags to go in there and wheelchair. So I made myself comfortable in the back seat by having a "neck pillow" and bobble hat on and a duvet over me. As we were going along my eyes opened up and I was amazed to see the trees and buildings and passers by with smiles on their faces, and how easy it looked for them to just walk normally and move easily! I felt so relieved and happy to be out of that hospital and into the fresh air. However, it was only about 10 minutes until I fell asleep and when I finally woke up, we were at home. It was just an incredible feeling, just walking through the front door and sitting on my own sofa. What made me smile even more was big old Buster, bounding up to me and he gave me a big lick on the side of my face and he sat so close to me I gave him a big cuddle because I was sitting on the sofa and Buster was sitting on the floor I had to lean to give him a cuddle and when I did I just fell onto the floor because I had no strength and it didn't matter because Buster stood over me and kept licking me then he laid down beside me and we had a big cuddle.

During those 6 weeks of waiting to start my radio therapy was ok I started to feel better inside like I didn't have any headaches and didn't feel sick. It was good because my brother was staying at my house because he didn't have to go back to work or out to Afganitan. We had a laugh because I'm not used to seeing my brother as he is always on tour or at his army base so it felt nice but because we have only got a 3 bedroom house and with me in one room, my sister in the other and mum in the other there was no room for him to sleep so he used to sleep on a camp bed in the downstairs living room. In the mornings I used to wake up, he made me laugh because I wasn't one to sleep in or get up late so I got up about 7 o'clock most mornings with my mum helping me down the stairs. My mum would make me breakfast and a cup of tea. Because the dining room was in with the living room I was always waking my brother up but because of the steroids I was on I was just so hungry and used to eat loads of cereal, slices of toast and cups of tea. It made me laugh because my bro was still asleep and I bet he thought "ah he is only having a bowl of cereal and then going back upstairs" but no I used to have 3 bowls and I used to wind him up then he would finally get up, he'd put the bed away and tidied things up. Then I would start this exercise I used to do as a goalkeeper I did it with my mum but it was so frustrating because I couldn't do it properly but I just tried my best and I got on with it. I said to my mum I want to go into school and see all my mates and everyone. One week my mum rang up my school De La Salle and Dr. Curnock, the Headteacher said Arnie can come in and see everyone. The day finally came and I was so excited, I was even excited to put on my school uniform and actually go into school (this was really surprising to me as I wasn't the most keen of students, which I guess many teenagers are like). So we did go into school and I had the most amazing feeling as I went through to the reception and sat down when 4 of my best girl mates came out, gave me a big cuddle and said hello. That was really nice; we all had a chat, it was me my mum, Mr Curnock and my four girls. It was great, we were talking for about 10 minutes, then they went back to class. After this me, my mum and Mr Curnock were going around the school knocking on some of the class room doors of my year. Then we approached my science class and Mr Curnock went into the classroom and stopped the teacher and said to the whole class I have someone very special outside. I was against the wall then Mr. Curnock said come in so when I walked in everyone stood up and clapped. One teacher I used to love came and give me a big hug and a kiss on the cheek, she bought me a bag of goodies, a Dr Hook, CD and a Dr. Hook, DVD, a Rocky sound track CD, two magazines and some muffins; all that stuff meant something to me.

The Rocky CD: we always had a CD playing in class. I went through her CD case once and found a Rocky sound track CD in there a put it on so from that day on every time I had that lesson the whole class would have to listen to it and as a new song came on my teacher would test me and say what scene was that song played and I always got it right.

The Dr Hook CD: As I have said I was, and still am, the class clown haha and I used to just get up and sing this in front of the whole class. Well in this lesson I sang Dr. Hook all the time.

The muffins : as I said I was cheeky and I didn't do as I was told to do. I didn't do my home work so my teacher would always give me after school detentions. She would just pick me up on something silly like talking in class or having my phone out or just messing about but I just think she fancied me because I was the only one getting after school detentions. So when I got there after school it was just me and her in the room and she had brought me some muffins and she would help me finish my work, but she was my best teacher.

Then I went to other classes where other of my mates were and I walked into the room and they all gasped, shouting things like "wahay Arnie's back", had a couple of jokes and laughs then I went up to the P.E department, said hello to everyone up there. As we were walking back my head teacher said its nearly lunch time, do you want to stay for lunch and have a chat to everyone? I said no sorry, I'm a bit tired but really my brother and sister were in the car and we were going down to Burger King and I was looking forward to it haha but now when I look back on it I wish I did stay for lunch. I think it would have been nice to get all the sympathy haha all the girls coming over but in the meantime it was just great to have my big bro about, going Burger King, going shopping him pushing me around in my wheel chair. Then a few days later we had to go to the local GP to get my staples and stitches removed from my head. This was strange because that is my local GP where the doctor told me there eas nothing wrong with me. It was just a strange feeling anyway I was having my staples and stitches out and I didn't really feel anything I was a bit scared but it was ok they came out pretty easily and I didn't feel anything. Then we came out of the nurses department and we saw my doctor walk past. My Mum then had a conversation with my him about what had happened and how he had mis-diagnosed me and all that had happened to me as a result of the way I am. She was saying to the doctor the way she felt because of the mis-diagnosis and she was saying that Arnie had to go through major surgery and have intense chemo and radio therapy. Naturally my mum was pretty angry at the doctor and she did raise her voice to him but maybe that was because my mum was so scared and afraid of what had happened so we went home from the doctors. We spent the rest of the weeks just chilling out, watching TV and going shopping with my mum, brother and sister. It felt really nice to be together until the day I started my radiotherapy. It was nice I guess because I didn't have to go to school, I was with my mum and brother but my sister had to go to school which was a shame but still when it was late morning 'ish when I finished my breakfast, I did a bit of physio and from sitting down on the sofa watching a bit of SpongeBob (cheeky) my mum used to say right let's get dressed and ready so I'd go upstairs with my mum and I would just quickly go on the computer whilst my mum was running my bath and getting my clothes ready. Then my mum would help me get in the bath she used to wash me, which I have said it was embarrassing and frustrating because I knew what I had to do but I couldn't and my mum always sat in the bathroom and watch me just in case I'd slip and hurt myself. One time, my brother Bill was round and my mum ran my bath. When it was done, the phone rang so my mum had to get it so she said Bill help Arnie in the bath and my brother said yes no worries I will help my best bro in the bath, which he did and I didn't feel embarrassed because we were brothers.

By this time my brother had to go back to work but the good thing was he didn't have to go back to Afghanistan he just went to base which was in Colchester, England. A couple of days passed and every day I had people coming and going all my friends and family friends brought get well soon cards and gifts around. I remember one day what a great surprise my friends at school probably planned it and about 10 of them all came round about 4 o'clock ish when school had finished, they were all in their school uniform and then Charilie Flannary and Josh Dean walked into my living room with big smiles on their face and said "oi oi, you alright Arn" and they had both shaved their head in honour of my getting cancer and I thought that was so nice. Well as the evening went on we were talking and on the computer watching videos of my brother out in Afghanistan which I thought was really wicked to say "yes that is my brother." About 7'ish everybody seemed to go which was nice because I was getting tired but what a fantastic night that was. There were nights when the family would all sit around the dining table and have dinner together and I remember this one time when my left hand just kicked out and just knocked all my mums peas off her plate and they went all over the floor and my mum just laughed and said cheers Arn then we all laughed well I thought it was funny because when you think about it your either laugh or cry and laughter is the best medication you can get.

The weeks of freedom had come to an end and the next day I had my appointment to start my radiotherapy. I then had a consultation to show me around the place and the radiotherapy machine I had to be on, they also took me around to meet everyone. Many people spent their time speaking to me to give me reassurance and to tell me that everything was going to be ok, but I wasn't scared to start with until the doctors finally sat me down to ask me some questions. Due to me only being 13 years of age they asked whether I'd like to have sperm saved because the radiotherapy would have "killed" this off therefore meaning I would be unable to ever father a child. I did not want to talk about it at that point in time because the whole subject just seemed irrelavent to me as I was only young. I particularly didn't want to speak about it because as a teenager I found it quite embarrassing so went ahead and regrettably turned down the offer of saving my sperm. We then left, had a bite to eat, then we were on our way home.

A couple days later just me and my mum had to go up there to get my mask made, my tattooed dots done (an alignment of tattooed dots to pinpoint where to use the radiotherapy) and my hair shaved off, no one had told me that I'd have to under go any of it, so I went through with it mentally unprepared. I soon was transfered into a room. During the 6 weeks of waiting my hair started to grow back so when we were in this room they had to make my mask but because it had to be skin tight they said can we cut you hair off, because if I had had it done with my hair still growing by the second treatment my hair would have all fallen out and the mask would have been too loose so they cut my hair and then moulded this big bit of hot plastic over my whole head and top shoulders then waited for it to dry then cut two eye holes and two nose holes out and attached 5 clips to it so they could clip me to the bed, they said right come on then lets test it out so I had to go into one of the radiotherapy rooms which scared me a bit because I had to walk through it was like a tunnel corridor into this room that looked like a laboratory with all these's radiotherapy mask's and dull grey walls I then had to take all my clothes off and just leave my pants on then get on the bed then they put the mask on me then clipped me to the bed. This was because I had to stay in the same position at all times every day for 6 weeks then whilst still all clipped in they drew little dots on my upper chest, just above my belly button and just above my penis and on my left and right side just under my armpit, then without telling me the doctor had a needle and pierced these ink dots into my skin so they could line me up every day to make sure the radiotherapy is hitting the right spot and the same place over and over again every day.

That day I noticed that the radiotherapy department had a ipod dock in the treatment rooms but I didn't have an ipod so my brother took me and my sister to Lakeside shopping center in Essex that night to buy me a ipod.

During shopping at Lakeside, my Mum rang my brother and asked if we could go home because she thought she had broken her ankle. We rushed back as soon as possible and we found my Mum lying on her bed in real pain. She explained what happened that she was laying in bed watching TV and the adverts came on so she rushed downstairs to get a glass of water. As she came rushing back up the stairs taking two steps at a time she missed a step and landed with her ankle which broke and twisted into 180 degrees.

My Aunt turned up, and then took Mum to A&E at Basildon Hospital where she was x-rayed, told she had broken her ankle which was put in plaster and she was not allowed to put any pressure on it for the next six weeks. Obviously the next day I was due to start my radiotherapy 5 days a week for 6 weeks! Due to my Mum's broken ankle, my brother Bill who is in the Army had to "beg, borrow and steal" to get time off duty to come with me for the radiotherapy.

Chapter Four

STARTING TREATMENT

I didn't sleep very well that night, knowing that I had to start my radiotherapy the next morning. It's a lonely time when you are laying in bed on your own, with thoughts running through your head of what can happen. It's pretty scarey!

I was sleeping on and off that night and finally time went by and it was 6am. I had to be up and ready for 7am because my radiotherapy started at 10am. but because I lived more than a ten mile radius out of London the hospital transport said you have to be picked up 3 hours before your appointment.

It was a strange feeling of leaving my Mum for a whole five days without seeing her but before I knew it me and my brother were all packed up and I gave my Mum a big kiss and cuddle goodbye. I said I would see her on the weekend, and off we went.

I arrived at University College London Hospital and went up to T12, which is a ward for just teenagers who are suffering from cancer. This is run by a large charity called Teenage Cancer Trust. I was all booked in and they showed me to my bed, I got everything sorted out and we had to wait until a porter arrived to take me to radiotherapy. When I go to radiotherapy a good thing about it was I didn't have to wait in the main waiting room – they sent me through to the childrens' waiting room where there were computer games and a lady who was a play specialist and after the meet and greet I was shown what was in the games room, we sat down to do some arts. She asked me what is your favourite colour and I told her orange. Then my brother whispered in my ear, saying you should have said something difficult like "magenta or sunset yellow". I thought it was funny but didn't say that so she gave me the orange piece of paper and she then asked me to draw a treatment chart so I tried to draw but because I had to swap hands because I couldn't use me left hand due to the op, I asked my brother to do a drawing for me so he drew a sketch of a person with wiggly hair. There were 30 wiggly hairs which was my 30 treatments, I had to put a sticker on one every time I had treatment.

Half hour later me and my brother went in for my first course of treatment. As I was walking through the dull, grey tunnel into what I thought was a labotory, they then told me to take my clothes off and just leave my boxers on I was about 8 stone at this stage. I laid on the bed and they put the mask on me and then clipped it down to the bed. As I was not able to move, I said to my brother put the ipod on shuffle, then he said he would see me in about 45 minutes.

As the nurses and my brother went to walk out, the nurses put a walkie-talkie by my side so that I could still talk to my brother. They all went into the office and said over walkie-talkie "we are going to start". This big machine was revolving around me and this was the start of the treatment. It was funny because my brother was pretending to be Rambo on the walkie-talkies and he was saying "my name is John Rambo, name your first blood". As he could see me from the office from the camaras, he said to me "move your right foot" and because I was strapped down and couldn't move, it was difficult for me to work out my left and right. I then moved my left foot and then my brother said to me over the walkie-talkie, "that was your left foot, you div"

It was hard to laugh in that very tight mask, but inside I was cracking up! I was relieved to hear from the walkie-talkie that they had finished that session.

Then I heard the wonderful sound of footsteps coming back into the room and the nurses were unclipping my mask, then I felt so relieved, got off the bed and got dressed and put the first sticker on my chart.

This was one down, 29 to go........

We then went up to T12 and it was like our home. I got on my bed and my brother got on the armchair and we were watching t.v.

We then went into the kitchen which was just like a family kitchen with patients and their parents and we were chatting and have a cup of tea. From there we used to visit the games room where we did arts and crafts, played pool, play station and an x-box and listened to music on the big 50" t.v. That was in the games room.

Then we were told that we were moving into an hotel because I wasn't ill enough to stay in a hospital, but it saved going all the way back to where I lived in Basildon and coming up again every morning.

The hospital supplied and paid for the hotel, which was 2 minutes away from the hospital. It was called The Grafton Hotel. We went down to the cafe in the hospital and my brother went out for a cigarette in the cafe the walls where all glass windows so you could see out and I was sitting right next to the window and he knocked on the window where I was on the other side in the cafeteria and started smiling and looked very happy whilst pointing over to The Grafton Hotel which was only over the road. My brother came in and we soon ran up back to the ward and packed our stuff as quickly as possible to get down into that fantastic hotel. We then walked through the doors of The Grafton and it was all marble floors and chandeliers. Because we were early to sign in we waited in the bar/restaurant area. We were sitting waiting there on the sofa and out of the blue, we fell asleep! Before we knew it., it was 4/5 o'clock and then my brother went up to the Reception and signed us in. We then went up to our room and it was amazing, very suave and sophisticated. Then we unpacked and went back out to get something to eat. We went down Tottenham Court Road and went into a Tesco Express and just bought a few sandwiches and crisps and nibbles. We then went back to the hotel and just sat there and watched t.v.

We woke up the next morning and I felt a bit sick. I had a bath and washed my shaved head. I then looked down at my hands and noticed there were tiny hairs in my hand. This didn't bother me, so I just washed my hands and thought to myself "pick yourself up, dust yourself down and start all over again" but of course I felt sad but I just got on with it and away we went.

We then went to the hospital, went down to the radiotherapy department which was good because as we was just allowed to walk past Reception and said hello and they would let me and my brother through and we went and sat in the games room and played wii console and did some arts and crafts and waited in comfort until I had to go in. We finally went in and they got me all ready on the bed which I didn't really think about it that much because it was good having my brother there because he used to make me laugh and kind of forget about the bad things about it. Then as I was strapped in I told him to put the songs on the I pod and then they all walked out. It made me laugh because my brother used to say "see you in a bit John", meaning "John Rambo".

I would be lying there with the music on and the radiotherapy machine going around me, it is funny because the nurses said to me that everyone explains a different smell but for me it smelt like "tomatoes". As I was just laying there relaxed, I heard from the right side of my ear, "are you OK in there, Rambo?" This was my brother talking to me from the walkie-talkies!

It then finished because it was about 10 o'clock in the morning, we didn't really have anything else to do so we used to spend our time up in the T12 ward in the day room playing pool and doing arts and crafts, and just generally talking to everyone like they were family.

We finally leave about 5pm on our walk back to the hotel. We got back into the hotel, put our things back and then went down to Tottenham Court Road to see what I fancied to eat. I had so many options from McDonalds, Subway, sandwich bars and pizza restaurants to Tesco Extra. At the time I really didn't fancy anything, but whatever I did fancy, my brother used to get it for me. For example, bacon, lettuce and tomato sandwiches, nice jam doughnuts and crisps. So we would take them back to the hotel and I very rarely eat them. I really fancied that sort of foods but when I went to eat them, the bacon was too salty, the crisps were too hard. The crisps were too strong flavoured and the doughnuts too sweet for my sensitive tongue and mouth.

We would then watch a film or a couple of films and go on my brother's computer. Then I had a bath for at least an hour and a half because my body was aching and I did not feel well. This was so relaxing, just to lay in the hot water of the bath. We would then go to sleep and wake up the next morning for breakfast in the hotel, which sometimes was hard for me to get up because I felt so tired, but I pushed myself to go up and get downstairs and have some breakfast. I would always fancy a full English breakfast, a slice of toast and a cup of tea. I just loved it looking down at the buffet breakfast and I could see the eggs, the bacon, the toast and even the cereals and the fruits that they had on offer and I always used to put something on my plate, but never would eat it. I physically could not eat it because I had no appetite, which was so frustrating because it all looked so nice.

We would then go back to the hospital and have my treatment and then go up to T12. So it was a pretty much day-to-day project of the same old thing. Unfortunately we only stayed in the Grafton Hotel for a week until the receptionist, John, whom we got to know very well, said to us because my brother could push me about in my wheelchair we were not allowed to stay at The Grafton as it was so close and for only people that struggled to walk a far distance could stay there. We were then moved to a new hotel, which was about half a mile away from the hospital which when we got in there was I don't know "different, I suppose". In my view, because I don't think the hotel redecorated from the late seventies!

What this hotel looked like was "dusty, salmon-pink carpets and walls with all old furniture". It also smelt old. When we went to our room, the room was no different, although it was quite big but I then looked into the bathroom and there was no bath, there was just a shower. So I said to my brother to go down to Reception and say that we needed a room with a bath. They changed us to another room which must have been the size of a box, but it had a bath! So we got settled in and this time, as luck would have it, there were a few more shops, bars and shopping centres nearby. So that night we went up to the high street and we had a look about and then my brother asked me what I fancied to eat. I said, I did not know.

So we went into a Tesco Extra and we just bought some sandwiches, crisps, sweets, doughnuts and coca cola, which pretty much every young teenager likes to pig out on, but not me as it used to hurt my mouth and I did not have an appetite.

We used to get home and just do what we usually did, watch tv, played on the computer and spent my long hours in the bath tub. Then, the next day began..... the same old regime for five days a week, for six weeks.

I had my ups and downs, funny days and boring days. Every day my brother could see I was losing weight so he said to my consultant, "my brother is not eating or drinking anything, and I am getting worried, so can you think of something to do" but she did not really come up with an option. I was just losing more and more weight.

A week later I had an appointment with my Consultant so we went to that appointment and as I got into the Reception I turned the corner and there were my Mum, sister and Auntie. They had got a taxi up just to see me. I was so happy and I had tears in my eyes because I didn't like spending too much time away from my Mum. It was sad to see my Mum hobbling along on her crutches because she was unable to put any weight on her leg. We were then called in to see my Consultant and then I was not really listening because I did not want to hear all the bad news but then I vaguely heard the doctor say "we need to do something drastically about Arnie's weight" because it has dropped so much in a short amount of time. My brother stood up from his chair quite drastically and I guess he did not mean to be horrible, but he got the hump and started shouting then walked out! He said something like "you could see my brother losing weight every single day, I asked you to help me and come up with some idea, and you didn't and now you are telling me that we need to do something drastic". I guess that really wound him up. We went back to the hospital, I had my radiotherapy and then I went up to T11 (T11 is the same as T12 but for younger children) but I was only there for a couple of hours.

Because I had to start my small dose of chemotherapy which was fed through my "pick line". That day was nice (I guess) because I was laying on the bed watching tv with my brother, sister, Mum and Auntie, who had all come up with me. Then my Auntie and sister went down to Macdonalds and got us all dinner. Then we were all eating this, except for me, because I was just chewing on a couple of chips. Then I sadly heard them say "we have got to go now" and then they went.

This was not bad because I still had my best brother there with me. It was about 5 o'clock when this finished and we went up to T12 and sat in the day room because we heard that Leona Lewis was coming up. We were sitting in there for a while and there was an easel with a piece of paper on it and I painted "we love you, Leona"and then my brother was saying "when she comes in shall we sing "just keep bleeding" the first line of her song to her, which I thought was really funny, but time was ticking over and eventually it was about 6 o'clock and I was getting tired, and Leona did not turn up.

So sadly I had to go because we had to make the walk back to the hotel before it got too late. We stopped at Macdonalds and my brother got me some chicken nuggets. I ate about two of them and I said they are really nice, so he made me eat another three, and he went up to the counter and bought some more to take back to the hotel because I liked them! As usual, they just got left because I did not fancy them any more.

It was the same old, same old, back at the hotel. During the night I fancied a fruit salad. It was about 9 o'clock and luckily enough, Tesco was just around the corner so my brother went out to get me one. He got back and I ran a nice hot bath. I jumped in it and it was just so relaxing and I just sat in there and ate my fruit salad.

I was looking forward to the next day as it was a Friday, and everyone loves a Friday, but for me I had my session of radiotherapy, then I was allowed to go home for the weekend, which was great to see my Mum and my sister. It was nice for me, my brother and Mum and sister to all be together, just going to Tesco, going out to Pizza Hut, coming back and watching t.v. and my Auntie used to pop around as well. It just great to be back together as a family.

I remember one time we were having dinner indoors and I was sitting next to my Mum at the dining table and she was on the left side of me and for some unknown reason my left hand just moved very quickly, knocking my peas of the plate and hitting my Mum in the arm. We all stopped and then we just started laughing. Saturday and Sunday were good days!

Sunday night we went to sleep knowing that we had to get the transport back to the hospital the next day. We got up and my brother packed his bag and my Mum packed mine. It was funny to see my Mum packing my bag because as she had a broken ankle which she was not allowed to put any weight on, she was moving around on her bottom!

The transport arrived on time and I had to say the 'awful goodbye' to my Mum and sister as me and my brother made our way to London for another week. We used to turn up at the hospital say our hellos at T12 and used to leave our bags up there, go down to radiotherapy, say hello to everyone down there, play in the games room and then I used to get called in to have another session.

This was the same routine for the next five days.....

Again, there were good days and bad days. I remember during this week, my platelets dropped so I had to go in and have a five hour blood transfusion which at that time I found out that my blood group was B positive. When I heard that it was an angel in disguise telling me "to be positive". There were fun times where radiotherapy used to finish early and me and my brother would have the whole day to do stuff. It was just fun to be wheeled around by my brother, going around Russell Square, down the streets where there were shops, pubs, etc. Then we found an outdoor shopping centre which looked very "posh" which had a few restaurants, also an HMV shop and a Waitrose. We used to go into HMV and look at the DVD's to see which one we would buy to watch that night. Then we would just get a film. On our way back we would go into Tesco and have a look around. There was a lot of lovely food from doughnuts to crisps and sweets, sandwiches and savouries which was very tempting for me, but I just couldn't eat them!

Then eventually, after about half an hour, I finally chose a sandwich. Then me and my brother bought a box of doughnuts to take back to the hotel.

I finally felt relieved as I walked through the hotel doors and I just felt I could relax. So we went up to our room and I just laid on my bed and put the t.v. on as this was a regular occurrence for me and my brother to watch Hollyoaks and The Simpsons. After the Simpsons, I would get in the bath.

It may sound strange to others but there I was just laying back, eating the doughnuts and the fruit salads and drinking milk shakes in the bath. It just felt amazing to me, the lovely hot water. I used to spend at least an hour and half in the bath and sometimes I even used to let water out and re-top it with hot water because, as you can imagine, after an hour and a half, it used to go a bit cold!

Then I just used to lie in bed, watching t.v. and fall asleep, just to wake up the next day to have another course of radiotherapy.

"Every night when I got back to the hotel, I felt drained and so I just loved to go and lay in the bath full of hot water because it felt so relaxing. I used to spend at least an hour in there at a time. I even had baths at 2 or 3 o'clock in the morning because I woke up aching and feeling and sick".

Going up to T12 and seeing everyone up there, including the Mums and Dads, the patients, the doctor, the nurses – it all just felt like a home away from home as they were all so lovely but unfortunately it wasn't. One night me and my brother were walking through the ward to go and see everyone in the day room and one of the nurses came up to us and said "Arnie, do you support Arsenal and I said yes so she said "do you want to go to a game tonight and I was like "What!!" I was so gobsmacked and I said yes straightaway. So me and my bro didnt go to the games room we turned around and went straight back to the hotel where we had a cup of tea, got changed because we had like an hour till kick off! As luck would have it there was a train station very near our hotel and then to get to Arsenal was like 25 minute train ride and we were there. Luckily I was in my wheelchair because it was a 8 o'clock kick off and we were running a bit behind and rushing though the train stations but we finally got there and we went to the box office where my brother asked for the tickets for Arnie Higgs and carer. They said yes so they walked us through all the behind the scenes areas and went up in the lift to I think the 3rd floor where we got out. This was my second time I had been at the Emirates stadium and on the 3rd floor it all looked so posh and they walked us though top quality box stands and me and my bro walked in this room to meet all these lovely people and then I stepped out the door and saw this magical green football pitch with all the lights and fans and music and I was just amazed! We then sat down and they gave us all blankets and made us all a hot drink. Half time came and we all went inside and when we were talking I found out that the people that were there was a charity called TEENS:)UNITE. So then they gave me a piece of paper and said what other stuff do you like doing, I then replied I love going to Arsenal games and concerts. My brother also wrote down what he enjoyed and as a huge West Ham supporter he stated that he loves going to watch West Ham play but only because he wants to go to all the West Ham games, we both found this very funny and amusing. (Obviously because my brother was my carer, he knew he had to come with me anywhere, so that is why he wrote "I love West Ham" on the piece of paper because if I ever got invited to West Ham, my brother knew he would have to take me so he would get the enjoyment of seeing his favourite team!)

We then watched the second half of the game, had a cup of hot chocolate and away we went back on the train. The train was really busy as everyone else was coming out but it didn't bother me because I was getting pushed around haha! After a 25 minute train journey we got back to our hotel and I was not hungry but was really thirsty so I said to my brother "can you make me a cup of tea" to which he replied "no do you want one of those protein shakes the doctor gave you" and I said "no" then my brother said "well I'm not making you a cup of tea". I then struggled to get up out of bed and went to make one. I got the cup out, put the tea and sugar in the cup and the milk as the kettle just boiled my brother said "Arn well done for getting up and doing it but I will pour in the water and walk it over to the bedside cabinct and I was like " cheers Bill, mate."

There were always times when I tried to drop my food on the floor for an excuse just for me to say "oh I can't eat that now and to look back on it now it is funny but I used to hide food from my brother because I lost my appetite from the radiotherapy, I did not want to eat anything so my brother kept asking me whatever I fancied he will get for me. So I did fancy everything that I saw, but just could not eat it so we then chucked it away. but one night I really fancied cold chicken on the bone so me and my brother got our hat, coat and boots on and went for a walk and I had a ride about in the wheelchair at 9:30 at night just to get this chicken so we did and when we got back to the hotel I had gone off of it, I didnt want to eat so my brother used to get in the shower and I opened the 8 piece chicken wings and shoved five of them under the bed mattress and when my brother came out of the shower I would say "look Bill, I ate 5 of them" and he was so happy with me I later on about 3/4 years later told my brother what I did and he was laughing and had a go at me and he said what must the cleaners think seeing chicken, sandwiches. fruit salads all hidden away in a hotel.

There was another time when my brother got me a BLT sandwich and this time he went out for a run around the block so I took the sandwich out the packaging and threw it out the window. By the way the curtains were shut at the time so when he got back I said I ate all the sandwich. He was really happy for me then after having a 2 hour bath haha me and my brother went to sleep not to know the next morning we woke up and when my brother opened the curtains, would you believe it there was my sandwich which I said I had eaten, it was sitting smack bang on a window flower box and my brother turned around and he wasnt happy and he told me off but still to this day I laugh about it but my brother dont haha.

And some times there were nice times when me and my brother were just together While we were in the Hotel, it was nice to spend that time with my brother just relaxing, watching films and playing on the computer because my brother was in the Army I didnt get to see him that often and it was just great to spend all that time with him but sadly it had to be in that situation.

One morning we woke up for breakfast. We were sitting down at the table and I had just finished a little bowl of cereal. I was sick, but able to keep it in my mouth so I left the table and my brother asked me what I was doing? I could not reply and just ignored him as I walked off to go to the bathroom. I didn't realize where the bathroom was so I ended up walking quite a while in this hotel. I finally found the toilet and just had to spit it all out into the toilet and wash my mouth out with water!

There were also times where amazing things happened maybe not to everyone else but I was really happy when one day me and Bill were in the President Hotel, we were down having breakfast and I did not notice but I looked up at my brother and he had a big smile on his face and I just looked at him and said "what's the matter?" He replied, "look, you are holding your knife and fork properly".

It is strange because I did not realize it just sort of came back! Just like that This only happened to me once and it was the last day of my treatment and I woke up that morning and I said I am going to walk to the hospital it was only approx 100 metres away from the hotel but I did it and I was determined, I was walking down the street pushing my wheelchair, my brother walking behind me and there were split second times where I thought to myself "ah I am so tired and out of breath" but then I just said come on lets do it, just one more push dont be beaten, no pain no gain and before I knew it there I was at the hospital. My brother didnt talk to me as I was walking as he said he could see how determined I was to do it and how concentrated I was but when I got to the hospital I said can you push me now and he said no you get up to T12 then I'll push you so I did it and I didnt complain I just got on and dealt with it then when we got there he said well done Arn and gave me a big cuddle. I later on in life learnt tough love it is where your family and friends love you so much they dread to see you in a bad state so they try to get you to do as much stuff as possible to get better. I guess it is called motivating others and I mean everyone can do anything thing they want to do but it is up to them if they want to do it, everybody could roll up in a ball and cry and feel sorry for themself but there are a few of us that dont want to and we want to inspire those who can't.

So me and my brother carried on with our day of the same old same old we see everyone up at T 12 then down to radiotherapy played in the games room and then went through to the old science laboratory put on the same songs and just laid there and then came out and then tried to have a milk shake or a bit of brunch but just didnt fancy anything so my brother tried to shove a chocolate bar down me haha. Most days my appointments for radiotherapy were at 9 o'clock in the morning. We normally waited for about 15 minutes and the radiotherapy took half an hour and then getting ready afterwards was about ten minutes, so all in all it was only about an hour so by that time it was about 10 o'clock and that was the end of our appointments. We used to think of what to do so we had days out and went to the Natural History Museum, the Science Museum and the London Museum.

And me and my brother used to go up Tottenham Court Road my brother used to be pushing me in the wheelchair and every time we went past this restaurant called "Eat" my brother used to tap me on the shoulder and go, "eat", meaning that I have to eat haha.

Another day as we were walking up Tottenham Court Road I noticed there was a little market stall (which I thought was a market) so I looked back at my brother because he was pushing me in a wheelchair and I said to him let's have a look in the market as I do like a little look and he said, yes, okay. As we were coming up the market was getting closer and we eventually reached the market but all it was was a five foot by eight foot stall selling hats and scarves!

So we just started laughing, saying that was the biggest market I had ever seen, I dont know why but we only walked up and down one side of Tottenham Court Road but it was just great to spend that time with my brother..

And sometimes after my radio appointment we would see the physio she used to walk up behind me and just say "I could tell that walk from anywhere but your doing really well". There were times when I did go down to the hospital gym with my physio and do a little bit well I guess I didnt want to do it because little things to other people like walking and balancing didnt mean anything to them but it was realy frustrating for me and I was just too tired sometimes to do the exercises but I had to do them and I did.

It finally came to the end of my radiotherapy treatment which I was very happy about. I received a certificate congratulating me on finishing the course and they also asked if I wanted to keep the radiotherapy mask and chart which I replied yes, just to be polite. As luck would have it we were only 5 minutes away from Oxford street and due to it being around Christmas time, my brother and I had the pleasure of being able to watch the lights being switched on, it was so beautiful and magical to hear the Christmas music and see the stunning glistening lights, it seemed like the time was perfect, was almost like a sign hope. Later on that week I took the radiotherapy mask home and into the upstairs of my house in which I started to really let my relief and happiness show, I started destroying the mask, this made me feel good, made me truly feel like at that second it was the end to it all. Even though I felt weak physically I still managed to balance myself by holding onto my stair bannister whilst crushing it with my feet. I then ripped up the radiotherapy treatmebnt chart too.

I had a couple of days rest at home until me and my mum had to go back to the hospital for another dose of chemotherapy. That night at the hospital in T12 half of the Arsenal football team came to visit and surprised us all with presents! We were sitting in the games room and they had Christmas gift bags and were calling peoples names out one by one and giving them the big bag of goodies. I was sitting there in amazment from just looking at the players but was more hoping that they'd call my name out for the goodies and just as I thought about it, they did!!! I was going through the bag and unwrapping the presents and we was all sitting there talking.

About an hour went by and they had to leave and so the patients, nurses, footballers and me all got a picture together which was put on T12's wall. That was a great end to the year.

Every time I had my little dose of chemo Vincristine I had to stay in hosptial for 3 days. As it was a Thursday I was looking forward to going home on the Saturday but on the Saturday afternoon the head nurse came up to me and said we are doing a charity video at the Arsenal training ground tomorrow morning so I said "oh my that is great and she said would you like to come, and I replied "that would be fantastic". I told her I did not have any clean clothes with me so she said that is no problem as you were supposed to be going home today, you can get into the the hospital transport car which will bring you straight back. So me and my Mum left everything at the hospital and went home to get some clean clothes. As we opened the front door of our house, what a great surprise it was as my sister had put all the Christmas decorations up, which looked so magical!

So we gathered ourselves together and jumped back into the transport car which took us back to the hospital. I jumped in the bath at the hospital and tried to have something to eat, got into bed and watched a movie and slowly fell asleep about eight o'clock. When we woke up on the Sunday morning about six o'clock, because it was so early I was really tired and I had not slept well that night so I did not feel too well in the morning. But because I was so excited I pushed myself and even ate a small bowl of cereal and got ready for the private hospital transport that came to pick us up at 7am and we arrived at the Arsenal ground.

I was looking out of the window to see all camera crew outside. We then sat inside with everyone else and were having tea and cakes and then I noticed that my favourite goalkeeper Manuel Almonia was walking past so with a surprised face I quickly looked at my Mum and said to her "there he is". This was incredible because just the night before we had been having a conversation about meeting him!

Because my best mate, Jack Chester, was a goalkeeper himself he must have already spoken to and knew Manuel. So Manuel brought out a pair of signed goalkeeper gloves for him. I asked my Mum to ask the Teenage Cancer Trust workers if I could meet him? So they came over to me and said, yes of course you can. They took me through and up the stairs to where he was getting ready for the video. I then saw him face to face and because I was so overwhelmed I had never been so quiet. So he went to put his big hand out to shake my hand.

I then went back downstairs and I said to my Mum I really wish I had given him a big cuddle. So we carried on with the day of filming and then a couple of hours later it was my turn for my part in the film which was to get everyone out of the van and rush them into the training ground and then pushing them all into a Masarati Sports car as Bachery Sagna?? was the chauffeur. I was getting tired by this point so I sat inside with my Mum as she must have felt tired as well. Whilst I was sitting inside, the Arsenal football TV channel came up to me and intrreviewed me which was great and then somebody must have told Manuel how he was my idol because he came out and gave me a signed goalkeeper's shirt and we had loads of pictures taken together.

Before the day came to a close, I ended up going back to the hospital as I was really tired. I had a little sleep and then the hospital transport took us home.

We then finished off the year with a lovely Christmas of me, my mum, brother and sister and a great New Years Eve. I remember it was New Years Eve night and I was tired so about 10 o'clock so I went upstairs to go to sleep. At 11:45 my brother came in to get me up to come and let off some fireworks at the park but sadly I remained in my bed as I was too tired. My mum stayed with me. Until this day I still feel out of order for making my mum stay and look after me as my brother and sister were having fun setting off the fireworks for new years. I then got told that they also all let a lantern off for good luck for me for the 'New Year'.

Chapter Five

THE POWER OF A POSITIVE MIND WHILST ON CHEMO

It was New Year, and I guess a new start to me having a lovely Christmas, as lovely as I could make it, as I was struggling to eat Christmas dinner and keep up with everyone partying and trying to have a good time.

The New Year started and I guess it was just a new start for me because it was the start of the chemotherapy and to feel better in myself as because I have achieved so much from the operation and the radiotherapy. I guess obviously it was sad going back to the hospital again to start chemo all over again, but in one sense it was good due to going up to T12 into the dayroom and seeing everyone again and seeing everyone was like a family and the play specialists, playing pool, and seeing my best mate, Jack, but this time it was different because obviously my brother had to go back to work at the army base. He was going to base in Ipswich, not to Afghanistan. My mum came with me which was really nice and I loved it. Obviously my Mum was still in her cast and crutches but she did her best and tried her hardest and it was fantastic what she did for me, although it was a struggle I had to help myself sometimes by carrying things and I did not give up or nothing like that and I motivated my Mum and she motivated me.

We were dreading going back to the hospital starting the chemo but went in the hospital around the 5th January and said hello to everyone and they showed us the bed and that was where it all started.

Unfortunately over the Christmas period I did not eat a lot and I lost a lot of weight, and after lots of discussion and meetings with my doctor, she finally decided to book an appointment for a feeding tube to go up my nose because I had lost so much weight which my brother was happy about and my Mum rang and told my brother.

We were up at the hospital on the Thursday in clinic, and after my brother Billy had discussions with the doctor about my weight that was going down and down, they decided to give me a feeding tube. They wanted to give it me on the Thursday but that evening I was supposed to be at school to collect my Award so the hospital transport collected us and took us home that night we went to my awards evening, because I started to go back to school full time I received an Award for Outstanding Achievement. When we were all sat down in the Sports Hall, Mr. Curnock, my Headteacher, opened the evening and started to give out the awards. It finally came to my Award and before he called out my name, he spoke a little speech, then I stood up for about two minutes and everyone stood up and clapped. Then I walked up onto the stage as everyone was still clapping, then Mr. Curnock shook my hand and said "all of this is for you, Arnie" (meaning the standing ovation). I looked to the audience and saw that a few people had happy tears in their eyes. I received my Award and then sat back down. As the evening was going on, I started to feel tired so I shook my head at Mr. Curnock and he knew I wanted to go so he said to everyone, "Arnie wants to go now because he is tired". As I was walking out, everyone was clapping me and as I was walking out one of my teachers, Mr. Paul Norris, stood up really tall and proudly shook my hand. Then I went home and had a good night's sleep. Then we were picked up first thing on the Friday morning and I had the feeding tube fitted on the Friday.

When I went back on the Friday, there was a nice family atmosphere with my Mum there beside me during the day and we were laying in bed watching films and we also got up and played pool and later on in the afternoon I had my feeding tube put in. They explained to me what was going to happen by putting it up my nose and down to my stomach which was obviously a strange situation for me because it had never happened before. I remember sitting on the bed at a 90 degree angle. It tickled at first and I could feel it at the back of my throat with the gag reflexes, the curtains were closed, there were about three nurses there and my mum was there and they finally pushed it in and then put a see-through plaster on my face, which I didn't like but finally they finished and after that I definitely did not feel like eating anything. Finally the nurse came and attached my first feed which was only for half an hour, but it was a big bottle which looked like a big litre bottle of milk. Obviously this had all the proteins and vitamins and stuff to help me. It felt strange and warm as it went up the tube. I guess it went as well as it could do actually. After a little while I got up and went to the toilet but after a while I got used to it. I don't think my body was taking it because after every feed I used to sick it all out. The time it took to finish my feed seemed like a waste of time because I kept sicking it up all the time.

As I only had to have chemo three days a week, we used to go home and I used to be like a vegetable or a coach potato because many a day I used to have to have my Mum help me in the bath, dress me and put my socks on. I used to sit there and watch t.v. I used to have a feed every hour actually so I started feeding at 12 and finished at 12.30 and be sick and get it everywhere. I used to sit at my computer, or have a little walk about a bit and then I had to go back to the sofa and start the feed all over again. What the doctors did not tell me was that the feeding tube would come out of my mouth when I was sick. What I had to do was everytime I was sick I had to pull it and this was a horrible taste of sick going up my throat and down through my nose. This went on for a period of six months and I was getting skinnier and skinnier and the doctor finally decided to put a peg into my stomach so I could be fed overnight as I was sleeping. I was then able to do more stuff in the day time. My mum tried to make me eat breakfast in the morning and I was full up because I was being fed overnight so that was why I didn't want the food during the day.

The operation to insert the peg was done with a small incision made into my stomach and I remember laying there and they put me out and my mum was beside me and I went into the theatre where the operation was done and I was brought back then fell asleep for about two minutes, I then woke up and wanted to know where this peg was. They told me it was in the middle of my stomach muscles, and my stomach muscles were really hurting me. I guess my Mum did not know how to use it as it was the first time she had ever seen one of those feeding machines. After two or three hours I was allowed to go home. I was kind of pretending to cry and panic because I wanted to stay in hospital as I didn't really feel comfortable for my mum to be doing this, but it was pretty easy and the nurses showed my mum and I how to do it and we went that night.

I was standing by my bed and the milk was clipped on and I did not feel any liquid going into my body. It was a bit uncomfortable sleeping and I was wary of which way to turn. Finally I got used to it and I had a good night's sleep actually to be fair and I woke up in the morning feeling energised. I felt a bit healthier because obviously I was starting to get my vitamins into me.

Obviously because it was overnight it was a large bottle of feed which filled me up more than ever.

I guess you are wondering why I have not mentioned about my Dad, because due to my Mum and Dad splitting up when I was a young boy, they didn't really talk a lot. When I was unwell, my Dad got really ill, stuttering, panicking and he was going to the doctor at that time. Really and truly he could not face the fact that one of his children was really ill and he could not stand there and look at me.

After a while, by this time I was getting a little better and my Dad started to come to come round and we started to go out. My Dad's way of getting over things was to go down the gym, to pump iron or only little weights or no weights, just do the movements or swim. Obviously this just lets off your anger or your sadness and lets off a lot of steam. I remember the first time my Dad felt a bit better he came around to see me and gave me a necklace with two boxing gloives on it and the reason for this was that Rocky's trainer gave him a necklace with two boxing gloves. He said that there is a little

This is where it all starts. My Dad, my sister and I used to go out on many trips, just to Southend to have a little walk around, but at this stage I was really skinny and just did not feel like doing anything. I was offered a wheelchair from a disability shop, which I used sometimes, but my Dad never let me use it. He always used to bring it in the van or the car, but my Dad said when we walk along the roads or the path in the High Street, you can always hold onto my arm. I was really weak and had no balance. He told me that we could sit down and there were times when we walked about 20 steps and I had to sit down. My Dad said he would always carry me and never wanted to see his boy in a disabled state. It was constant at this time, I was having the chemotherapy. I cannot lie and you can't make yourself feel big by saying it, there were times where I was in bed and I would wake up my Mum and I would feel sick and I was scared of what was going on. You are laying there with the curtains closed and I remember being sick and the nurses used to come and help me and give me water. This was a terrible time, but I guess it was just a thing you had to get on with. When you are on your own without your true friends, I guess it is a lonely time and you think "why me" and you wonder what is going to happen. Everyone must do this, no matter how hard you try not to think about it obviously it is always there. My Mum did everything for me in the morning, she used to ask me if I wanted tea and toast. She was worried about me and she used to get my bath ready for me. I used to have bubbles in the bath. She was always there, like an angel, no matter whether I felt sad, or felt mad. It sounds strange because obviously I love my Mum dearly, but just for those splits seconds my life or my freedom in that short time. We used to go to the day room and they had a massive DVD collection and obviously we uswed to watch a lot of DVD's. It was sad to be in that situation, but no matter what time it was, if I told her I fancied a packet of crisps or a milkshake she would always go and buy me whatever I wanted, despite whether she was reading a magazine or doing something she would give up her time to help.

In March/April, my pick-line in my arm became infected. It did not hurt but obviously the nurses came around every Friday to give it a clean to make sure there was no infection. It goes all the way through the vein in the bicep to the tip of the heart. I had to wear a plaster and as this was the tube that was feeding the chemo into my body, it was all red around where the incision was and there was scabbing and they told me it was infected. I was not expecting this and they had to take out the pick line which was really, really cringing. I was laying on the bed and they were pulling out the tube like they were pulling a worm out of its hole in the ground. They then cleaned the wound and the hole up and put another tube in the other arm.

It was really scary. I did not make a big scene about it because I pretended that nothing hurt me. They told me they would put a needle in my arm. This process lasted about two hours and I was on the ward in the T12 unit and the lady put a hole in my left bicep.

My right hand was grabbing the mattress of the bed and I was gritting my teeth and my Mum was standing there and she could see everything that was going on. Obviously I could still feel it in the vein and it was just such a scary feeling, and you can imagine a four stone boy lying on the bed and I was crying and not really crying, but when I used to go into the hospital I used to qact as a clown and never showed any sad emotions. I always thought that I was the person that everybody had to look up to. I always had that feeling of "Mr. Motivator" because I was so positive on the ward and so chirpy, I used to be like "hello, darling are you all right?" to all the nurses. My mum tried to take my mind off it by talking to me and trying to make me laugh.

It was about 45-50 minutes they were pushing the tube up my arm and they finally came to the conclusion that it was not in my vein. Obviously I wasn't happy about that, but after about 2 hours later it finally went into the vein. It was wrapped up in a bandage ready for the next chemotherapy. It felt more sensitive because it was in my left arm. This was the arm which I broke when I was about ten years old and I had no feeling in the bottom part of this arm. Also, due to the brain operation I have no co-ordination in this arm which makes it much more sensitive.

We finally packed our bags and the transport picked us up and took us home. It was about 4-5 hours it felt uncomfortable but I got used to it after a while.

Life went on and I was continuing with my day-by-day treatment sessions, and I remember one day when me and my Mum finished a week dose of chemotherapy, I came home and just as I walked through the front door, my Mum's boyfriend said, "I have to take "Buster" to the vet (Buster was about 13 years and his back legs went) and you will have to say goodbye, but at this time I wasn't that well and I was not feeling great as I had just got back from my three day chemo sesh and it was the first time I had to do something like that so I was sitting on the sofa and I just lent over and gave Buster a big cuddle and said "I love you, Buster". So off he went and he didn't come back because he was put down. Obviously I was only a young and ill boy at the time and I didn't really know 100% what was happening but then I found out he was put down I was distraught. Now, as I am a young man, I realise things what to do and not to do and I believe in never putting a good dog down. I mean Buster was all there in the head,

Buster had a great heart and great health. It was just his back legs, the way I look at it is if a human being maybe at the age of 35 or 40 and becomes paralysed in their legs or arms or from the chest down, you would not kill them or put them down you would do all you can to love them and care for them and either think of ways to maybe be them in a wheelchair so why not do that to a loving family dog! Since that day, I despise that man for killing my dog.

There were many trips along Leigh beach with my Dad seeing how far I could go and what I could do. Me, my Dad and my sister went down to Rossi's ice cream in Southend and we all ordered an icecream in a cone. On the way outside I dropped mine on the floor and I was angry about this and my Dad said to me "oh, well better luck next time". My Dad did not used to show any sort of sympathy to me, obviously he really cared about me but this was a good attitude from him which I liked. My Dad and my sister were sitting there eating and obviously I did not have an ice-cream. There were two little boys about 9 years old, and they came running past and I was sitting there with my sister and my Dad, and my Dad said to me "here, Arn, you are going to be doing that in a year's time" and I thought, "yeh, I am going to do it and I am going to make my old man proud".

Obviously I did not say this out loud. It is those moments you cherish. Some people are not grateful for those sorts of things. When you are in hospital it is hot, but those times when you are sitting on a park bench looking at the sea, you just think I am so grateful I am here, so grateful I am healthy, and can smell the fresh sea air and the sun nice and warm on your head. There were other times when we did strange things which some people would not think of doing. My Dad made me wear a rucksack with a tin of beans in it every day, with an extra tin of beans in it. He did not tell me why, but it was like the film, The Karate Kid, where the trainer makes Daniel do something. In the end, obviously my posture started to get better as well as the strength in my legs and there were times when I was around my Dad's or at my house. My Dad used to tell me to put my chest out, shoulders back and there were times when I lost my balance, I could not ride a bike or could not run properly. My Dad brought around a three-wheeled tricycle for me so we went up to Langdon Hills in the area where I live where we used to bike ride there in the long hills and the long grass. This was to make my legs stronger, but if I fell off into the long grass, I would not hurt myself.

During the last three or four years, during my rehab, we walked around that field and even now I still get tired from walking long distances. However, I try my hardest to get to my destination. In my mind, I try to never give up. My Dad used to just stand there and he used to walk off about 20-30 metres and shouted over to me, "Arn, run". There is no word in my life such as "CAN'T". Obviously when my Dad said to me "run" I automatically did. I just did it. I ran like the wind blows. I did run ackwardly but I did run! All my legs were up in the air, and I looked like a brand new baby running for the first time and my Dad gave me a big cuddle. I carried on doing it pretty much every day. I only used to run from the bottom of my road to the top of my road, which is only about five houses, about 30 metres. I used to see if I could get better. I am not 100 percent perfect, but obviously I can do it.

There were times when my Dad told me to "walk on that bench". The first thing that comes into your head is that you think you can't do it.

It is an automatic feeling but my Dad put me up there and he was steadying me and I had my hands out like I was walking on a tightrope and my Dad said to me "well done, that's an achievement".

When I had my new "pick line" in my arm, I wasn't allowed to get it wet, and was not allowed to get the feeding tube in my stomach wet either. My Dad was so determined with me and I used to love swimming so he used to say to me "let's get some cling film around your arm so it doesn't get wet".

I used to go to my local gym, David Lloyd, and I used to swim. At this time I was still skinny and weak, my cheekbones were hanging out, I just looked like an alien. I had little aches in my arms and in my head and did not feel 100 per cent every day. I used to be like a clown with everyone coming up to me asking how I was, and I just used to say "I am all right thank you, I'm getting better every day". then I used to get changed to get into the swimming pool and walk the length of the swimming pool with my arm in the air and walk in the pool and it was quite ackward due to my poor balance but it was better in the pool. We used to do this every single day and I was not worried about getting the pick-line or the feeding tube wet, I just really wanted to do it.

The funny thing was although I was doing that for a long time, I never ever got an infection in either of them, and I always wonder whether that is due to the positive attitude I had and other people have told me that their pick-line got wet and became infected. I think I have had my pick-line changed once because it was in the early stages where I dropped my arm in the bath and it became infected, but all the times in the swimming pool, it never got infected. I didn't have any trouble with it at all and I believe that it is due to positive thinking!

At one point my Dad even paid to get me a personal trainer. Obviously my Dad has been doing gym and exercises and used to be on the TV programme "Gladiators". There was a feature in our local Evening Echo. He has always been a determined sort of person. I had this personal trainer for about two weeks. He used to show me how to walk on a stepping machine but he did not know my background. Obviously I could not do the two minutes on the exercise machine, and eventually my Dad came up and told him what was the matter with me.

My Dad took me over after this and we did little things like light weights and we were doing all the machines that are fixed to the ground because I did not have any balance because there was no way I could pick up a 5 kilo weight due to losing my balance. We did the movements to get the blood flowing and there were times when I went to the gym iun my wheelchair and I used to have ask them if I could go up in the lift. There were times when I was sitting indoors and my Dad would say, "come on Arn, let's go and do a 5 minute workout?" I used to say I don't want to go, and he used to make me go. I don't know how he did it, it was just the motivation he had to make me do it. He used to say ok, we will just go and have a shower and a swim!

We used to go up to the gym, and we used to do 5 minutes, which was better than nothing. Dad always worked me in the gym and the swimming pool. I guess he thought I was an Olympic athlete or a racehorse or something. If you can just imagine a bald, skinny boy, with his arm up in the air, wrapped in cling film! I can guarantee this every single time I said to my Dad, I don't really fancy going to the gym, every time I came out I would say to him, "I'm glad I came" and this was 100% of the time

Obviously when you are in the gym, you are meeting people and you feel better than sitting indoors. All this was duriing my chemotherapy and I was still weak and tired and there were many times when I was laying in bed and really sick and had headaches and there were times when I had headaches. There were such awful times, to be fair where I didn't feel myself, I just felt like skin and bones and felt weak all the time, but due to my Dad motivating me all the time I did not give up. One time, a social worker came to talk to me but although I did not feel I needed someone to come and talk to me, she came anyway and I was inspiring her and she smiled at me and said to me: "Arnie, I wish I could have what you have and put it in a little bottle and give it to other patients". Those kind of words stick in your mind for ever, and it made me feel good so I went on to help them.

Everyday I used to do something to help me with my rehab whether it was physio or occupation therapy or whether it was my dad getting me up the gym but I always used to do something, I never used to sit there and do nothing and majority of the time I wanted to stay at home or do somthing at home but my dad made me go up the gym. I always did it, I always used to go up the gym with my dad whether he spurred me on because there were times where I didn't want to go up there and he used to say to me alright Arn let's just go for a little shower or let's go sit up there and have a cup of coffee and just chill out up there and I used to fall for it all the time so we would go up there and go into the changing room, get ready to have a shower and he would always say come on Arn we'll go do 5 or 10 mins up there and it was funny because I never used to say 'ah na dad I dont want to go up there and do anything". Its funny because 100% of the time I used to come out of David Lloyd and say I am glad I went up there to do a bit in the gym, a swim and shower. I used to love it and the trouble is with all home gyms and home exercises which families get built in for their son, daughter or family member but it is bad because in one sense you are not getting out and your not talking to other people, or not keeping in contact with the outside life and more or less locking yourself away, being shy not wanting to see anyone or you dont want anyone to see you. It is all good buying all this new technology and equipment like cross trainers and everything like that to keep fit, but my views are it is best going down to your local gym, meeting other people and getting more confidence back and at the same time you are showing off your bald head, showing off your skinniness, showing off your fat ness or your spots or whatever and it is for those people down the gym who look at you and they think "cor look at her or him they are determind to do somthing" and I must say due to my dad that is what I have done from day 1 really, but there are those times when you do feel like giving up because nothing seems to be happening, nothing seems to get better or muscles bigger and all the hard work you put in but what you have got to remember is that nothing happens overnight, well nothing drastically happens overnight and it is just those little 5 minutes or ten minutes at a time of just doing little things like squeezing a tennis ball to build the muscle in the forearm or use a tin of beans and do bicep curls or getting a oven glove put a tin of beans in each side and put it on your foot, lean back and lift your legs. This all gets the blood flowing and stops the muscle from deteriorating, it is just things like that by doing the 5 minutes a day just makes the human body better and before you know it you start to feel better and little things like holding your knife and fork come back naturally but dont get me wrong, I have nothing against home gyms, they are really good and great you can do a lot more at home and feel like you dont care about what you look like because no one can see you but it is best to GET UP, GET OUT, GET MOVING AND GET MOTiVATED,

Of course there were times when I felt tired; felt that I did not want to do anything or whatever but when I tried to motivate other people I did not tell them to do something that I have never done. I am obviously the type of person to lay in bed, feel sorry for myself and then start getting up saying "come on boys, get up and do a swim, do some exercises, it is a false illusion, but obviously from then on what made me feel better was my hair started to grow back. Obviously this happened very slowly because it was the radiotherapy that killed it all off.

Let's say February/March time it started to grow back slowly which obviously made me feel better, more confident and whatever and obviously with the feeds, it started to make me feel stronger. There was a point where it was funny, and it took your mind off it. Me and the boys in T12, Nicholas and when old Jack was there and Stanley and everyone else there were loads of people, we used to walk about the wards with our bobble hats on and it was just great because we wore them because we were all bald but when I used to go out with my Dad, my Dad used to say to me "take your hat off, but I was like "no I do not want to do that" because I did not want anyone to see me this way I was and he was like "Oi, take it off and let the world see what you are going through and obviously show them how strong you are"

Obviously every day I was getting stronger and I cannot remember who it was, I think it was my Dad's mate who told me there was one wise man who said "you are like a car, you need to eat and if you do not eat you die, like a car if you do not put petrol in it, it dies".

It is the same with the human body, if it does not get food or drink you die. I do not know whether it scared me but since that day I started to eat a bit more, but not loads, obviously nothing like a full English breakfast, but I used to nibble a bit more. Maybe it was the effect of little and often.

Hint – it all comes down to the situation of proportions of food or maybe I really did not know the sizes of the meals, it was to kind of scare me in some sort of ways, "I cannot eat all that, I am not even going to try, but when I tried, which obviously is advice for you, the person reading the book, so that I used to have a saucer and fill it up with pasta, potatoes, but if you put that in front of your son, daughter or relative and they are scared of eating it would then be swapped onto a bigger plate so it looked like a lots because it is a question of "mind over matter". It is all psychological!

Then they may have a little go because obviously they feel better in themselves for eating something and gradually, gradually, it gets better, but it is very slow progress. It was a very slow progress but I tried and tried again and finally I Succeeded and carried on eating those little meals and eventually went on to eating bigger meals.

Obviously no matter how much you tried, it is well hard for a little while. I guess it is just the urge to feeling unwell or being unwell, I do not like it, you feel small and you feel timid. You just want to get it out of your mind about not eating but you cannot and get frustrated with yourself if you cannot do anything, you have just got to try and try again and obviously just let the time roll, let months roll, let years roll and this was extremely frustrating for me. I was probably about 70 percent better, but still felt a bit weak but it is just a matter of pushing yourself.

There was a time when I had to spend my birthday in hospital and it was frustrating for me because I could not see all my friends and family and celebrate it properly.

It was just fantastic. I remember sitting in the day room and my back was to the door, everyone was having a laugh, playing x-box or on the pool table. Me and my Mum were sitting down at the Arts and Crafts table and I was sitting there with the play specialist and we were talking and whatever and I noticed my mum go out of the room but I did not really take any notice or turn around and say "Mum, where are you going?" She went and that was it, and anyway the play specialist was talking to me and I was looking over at her and then behind me everyone kept quiet, even the other patients in the Day Room, they did not say anything but Manuel Almunia, The Arsenal goalkeeper tapped me on the back of the shoulder and I turned around and so I was like "who's that?" and I turned around normally and there he was and for that split second, I was surprised and amazed, I was so surprised, I just did not know what to do, I just started bursting out crying in surprise and happiness and it was just such an amazing feeling and I was giving him a big hug and I must admit I was cuddling him for at least 25 minutes until my Mum finally said to me "Arnie, you have need to let him go of him, you can't take him home"

I finally let go of him and I was crying and wiping my eyes and there was like a big photographer, a big camera crew there taking pictures and whatever and then I stood up and Manuel was there as well and he gave me a signed t-shirt, a signed football shirt. It was amazing, me, my mum and Manuel were talking for about an hour when at last he brought in a cake with candles on it, and we ate a bit of that. Then we played a game of pool and then I racked up and at the start of the game he said to me, "I bet you fifty pounds, if you win you get fifty pounds, so I said, "yeh all right then", and we shook on it and anyway we were playing pool and whatever, obviously it was hard for me because I could not see out of my left eye, my co-ordination in my left arm, it was all a bit ackward but I thought "nah, I'm gonna have this one", so anyway I was playing and I think luck was on my side that day because I potted all my balls and I only had the black left. Then Armenia took his shot and missed it and the white ball rolled into a perfect position for me to pot the black ball so I screwed back and hit the bottom of the white ball as hard as I could, and the black went straight in. There was the true moment of Manual Almunia handing me over a fifty pound note, a brand new one, all red and crispy. He shook my hand and I gave him a cuddle again (not for 25 minutes this time) and he said to me "Arnie, my friend, I am gonna wait until you get a little bit more better then I will invite you to the Arsenal training ground for a training session and I was so amazed I think maybe that was a bit of determination, just to play football, to play in goal with my idol and I guess from that day I was a bit more determined actually in life to get better. Anyway after that I guess life just carried on getting back to the treatment and the push to get to the Arsenal, to train and spend time with Manuel. Every day I used to do something to help with my rehabilitation, whether it was OT (occupational therapy) or whether it was physio or whether it was my Dad getting me up to the gym, I always used to do something, I never used to sit there and do nothing.

Rehab continued:

I had many things that helped me, for example, I had a balance board made for me because my balance was really bad. I noticed that there was a balance board in the physio department at the London hospital and I was using that in the hospital and I thought let me carry on from what I was doing at the hospital at home to see if I can get better at it and then I had one made by my auntie's friend who is a carpenter. He made this for me and I was using that for the time being and there was other equipment which was made for me as well. They were called foot ups. What they are is attachments to go round your ankle and go around your feet, they click together and bring your foot up into a 90 degree angle with your leg and ankle. Because obviously I struggled with footdrop which was due to the small doses of chemo that I had, half hour doses at my local hospital Basildon, every Wednesday. The footups were just to support my ankles because they just kept flopping down, I couldn't walk properly. I had to keep bringing my knees up really high to stop tripping over because my ankles just kept flopping. Obviously due to that the way I walk now is different to everyone else. It doesn't look that much different but the way the doctor explained it was that I am walking, where a normal person would walk with their knee forward and their hip back, I walk with my knee back and my hip forward, and this is strange but gradually along down the line when I was getting better and better each day I was coming to the end of the chemotherapy and I thought I don't need the foot-ups any more.

There was one more piece of apparatus that was made for me which was overnight splints. This was two plastic legs molded to the shape and size of my legs. They were plastic leg supports that used to go over my feet and go up to my knee and I used to have strap them in on both legs to stop my feet flopping forward when I slept at night.

Obviously it is natural thing that everybody does when they sleep on their back, their feet fall forward.

With me, it was worst and my calf started cramping up all the time so they were just there to support my ankles but at the end of 2010 I did not feel like I needed them any more and I started to give my stuff away to other people, Because I felt as if I didn't need my rehab equetment but really I did but inside I didn't care about my self I was just so determined to help others so I used to give it to them so they can use it and get better my journey carried on through the courses of chemopherapy and my little doses at my local hospital making all the nurses on the ward like me and not forget me in a way I was being a cheeky chappy by saying 'allo darling' or 'allo sweetheart' and just the norm or being cheeky but I guess they liked it because I was like a clown I showed that I had nothing wrong with me and I was laughting about it and didn't care about but it did bother me, there were many nights where I used to cry myself to sleep and get angry with myself because I couldn't do things properly or like I used to do like I wanted to run the way I ran, play football the way I played football, or even have the stamina to to out with my mates and walk about the way I used to do it for example walk freely, not be tired, not get a stitch, not be out of breath but I guess that all gave me more encouragement to get better and I heard this quote from my dad ; you laugh and the whole world laughs with you, or you cry and you cry alone. I mean every body has those low moments in life but I guess it is just when you are alone I mean I guess it was about August time when I thought to myself you are who you are and everything in life is done for a reason so just live with it and make it better so I did just get on with it and stopped thinking about the past.

I had a real fear of needles, I just hated them and still do I dont know whether it is because I have had so many but I just dont like them and this one day I had to go up to London to have one of many MRI scans and I can't remember if I woke up with the 'ump or if I was scared but I had a grumpy face all the way up there and before the scan they had to put a needle (cannula) in my hand this is for when they insert some dye into my body halfway though the scan this is so you can see the main organs more clearly in my case the brain, and as I was in not a good mood I said "just hurry up and put in my cannula" so the nurses said "do you want numbing cream or spray and I said "no just get on with it". So she did, it really hurt as she was putting it in I bet she couldnt find a vein so it was taking long time to put in and I was tensing my fist, gritting my teeth and I dont know why but started to cry. I guess it was all the build-up from being grumpy, just determined to get it over and done with because it really hurt. Then she said to me again "do you want numbing cream and I just said "no just get it over and done with and in the end with blood running down my hand the nurses finally did it and I was ok.

So after that I went on to have my mri scan, I felt as if everything was okay obviously i've had many MRI scans in the past but the I guess the reason I new that everything was okay was because that my first MRI scan I ever had was at the eye hospital in southend when I had the brain tumor still and we was there and had a bit of lunch. When I had the MRI scan and they inserted the dye into me, they then slowly moved me back under, but I had to push the panic button as I started to feel really sick, the doctors asked me if I could hold in until after the scan but there was no way I could hold it, They asked if I was sure but I really couldnt hold it, so they took the neck braces off and everything. I quickly turned to the side and I was sick all over the floor, I guess that was because the dye reacted to the brain tumor so everytime I have an MRI scan now and I don't be sick I know that everythings okay because the brain tumor isnt there anymore and I wasn't sick because the tumor asnt reacted with the dye. After that we went home and had to wait a week for my MRI results, it was just the same on the ward everyday, I was there with my mum and she was laying in the bed with me and I was doing what I was doing every day I would go to the games room say hello to the nurses, play a bit of pool do a bit of arts and crafts or whatever. My mum would be there with me, in a way I guess in one way it wsas nice, it was like a home away from home, especially spending all that beautiful time with my mum. The times of going to bed when all the blinds were shut and the windows closed all the curtains would be pulled round and the dim lights were on, your all like tucked in to bed, had a bath watching a film or tv and my mum being there right next to me and we would watch films or whatever and slowly go to sleep, I would wake up being sick due to the chemo, I guess thats how my days went for the poeriod of the time that I was having the treatment it slowly come to an end eventually by the time it was coming up to christmas and I had finished, it was December 1st and I had finish my chemotherapy and I guess that was the end of it, that day was fantastic obviously! I had my picc line taken out my arm but I still had my feeding tube in and whatever but it just felt so much more relief so you know what I mean you dont have to go back on to the ward again you dont have to have all the horrible treatment and whatever, it made me feeel so much better, christmas come and we had christmas parties actually with the teenage canccr trust and teens unite they would throw a party every year whether it was at some fancy church been done up.

There would be celebs, gifts, raffles, lovely food, lovely entertainment, a choir, singers it was really nice being in a happy place, everyone there laughiong and joking and I guess for those split moment everyone would forget why we there and why they were invited because it was such a great time and you didnt think about anything, you didn't think of the cancer and everything you were going through what I had noticed was a photographer there that used to take pictures he was a photographer who took a pictures with animated backgrounds, I remember you could pick whether you wanted to be in a snow globe or santas slay or whatever, back in christmas 2008.

I went to the christmas party for the first ever time I had picture taken there christmas 2009 I had my picture taken there as well. When I got home I put both the pictures together and I couldnt believe it I looked completley different person, obviously I looked healthier my hair was growing back I didnt have the feeding tube in my nose I guess even that made me more proud of my self. So I mean that was a plus I guess obviously christmas time was here it was a better christmas in 2009 obviously I felt so much better I was eating more, more treats chocolates, christmas cakes just lovely things like that, obviously by now I had my appetite back, my brother was back at the time which was a lovely christmas me, my brother, my mum and my sister all together and we went round my aunty Marlenes and go see my family and cousins, it was so nice all getting together and enjoying christmas and having the log fire on being all together as a family, yeah it was really nice, on the boxing day we would always me my sister and my dad would go to really early down to the shopping mall on southend high street, we would go out for the boxing day sales, we would then walk along the seaside have an ice cream or a coffee, in our winter coats, which I guess is really nice. So we get together every year now and do that, the new years started and I guess it was an exciting year to look forward to theres a charity called make a wish foundation which helps loads of children world wide with seriously ill ilness' and I guess they had granted me my wish which was to go to Florida to Disney Land, universal studios so I had that to look forward to which was in May 18th my birthday, I guess I was looking forward to a training day with Manuel Alumnia, the days would go by then the months as usual I was doing what I always do which was a bit of everything really goiing down the gym a bit of exercise goiing to school seeing my friends, I guess it was nice as in I felt alot better without no chemo tube in my arm not getting no treatment no more which made me feel so much better I had got my appetite back by now, it made me feel so miuch better, may time came that was birthday we had everything booked for the 17th no wait sorry we had the holiday booked for the 15th so we had left on the 15th, we had to stay in a hotel at stansted london for the night the flight wasnt until the next day, we had everything in a package from make a wish foundation there was £50 in for dinner that night at holiday inn I think it was, in the morning we woke up I was obviously really tired so we got the hire car from the hotel to the airport when we had got into the airport we had to go through all customs and what not, I guess that made more excited I find being at the airport fun, if your not a person to go on holiday all the time we finally got on to the airplane for a 10 hour flight, the plane was really nice had quite a bit of leg room had a snack bar the telly infornt of us, I just layed there for watched a bit of tv, listened to a bit of music getting crisps, chocolate and coke and stuff whenever the trolley would come up, it was nice but I wouldn't reccomend as any one would, that was a nice flight we finally arrived in florida, we was all looking out the window as were flying across america yeah it was just getting more and more exciting as we were getting closer as were going through the airport in Florida it was even more exciting it was a whole different place, as I walked passed the american shops I would see all the american sweets catch my eye the american food products and the magazines and whatever it was really exciting for me I was just over the moon, then we got outside went through doors and the beautiful hot weather just hit y we then got in to a taxi that took us to a car rental place, so we hired a car which make a wish foundation organised for us we then drove away which was strange because of obvioulsy there cars are left hand drive and they drive on the left of the road, which is opposite to us, again it was another like exciting moment it gave me a strange feeling, we set the sat nav to the place we were staying at and made our way there, we stayed at a place callled give kids the world village, as soon as we pulledc in to the gates they was it was like all little bungalows put together like everywhere and like they had everything you can think off they had it there, sports, basketball courts, swimming pools there was horse back riding, loads of stuff. There was a 24/7 ice cream parlour you could go every minute, every hour go get yourself an ice cream or a milkshake for nothing, There was a big events stage area, where every night they had disney characters like mickey mouse, minnie mouse, goofy, daffy duck etc. on stage, everyone would sit in there chair or whatever and they would do a big show, there was just so much there to do, everything a kid could think of was there, there was a massive park, cinema there, there was a special place there actually they made it out to be a magic cave when you go inside theres all gold stars on the walls and ceilings covered, at the end of the trip you put your star in a box and make a wish, they would then stick on a space in the cave, so every kid who had gone to the village has there star in the cave, so it would stay there forever, then this place you could just sit there was like secrets hiding areas for the little kid I guess, you could sit there and listen to some really wonderful music, that night we went back to our bungalow I remember it saying on there welcome home arnie, we then unloaded our suitcases we picked our rooms, got changed then we went out to the theatre area where there was a disney show on which was really nice, it was dark but it was really warm, there was a couple of lizards running about on the floor, fire flies, it was loovely.

It was nice and warm but humid, you was just walking about in your shorts, which was so much different to the UK, Do you know what I mean? It's a great time great experience which I guess you can only feel if you go out there, its better then you could ever imaginme, we got home that night we went in to our rooms and just chilled out really whatched a bit of tv, then went to sleep, when I was in my bed there was all duvet blankets that werent very thick, I only had one because it was so hot, in the middle of the night I woke up because it was really cold because the air conditioning in the bungalow area was on as it was so hot outside, I had actually woke up in the middle of the night, and shouted for my mum and asked her to put another blanket over me becuase I was really cold, so my mum come in put a blanket over me and I fell straight back to sleep,

I had a good nights sleep and woke up the next morning, had a shower got dressed and we went to the cafe area where they had what was like a buffet of breakfast, eggs, bacon, beans, your cereals, croissants, orange juice, teas, coffees, we would go out get what we wanted, I remeber there was this lovely lady there actually, everyone who works at make a wish foundation our volunteers which is such a nice thing to do, there was this one lady who I wouldn't say was down syndrome, special needs in her 70s, I took a charm to her cos she had smiled at me, i'm that kind of person where when you notice a smile and it makes you feel good and I like her I felt a good positive aura from this lady, so I went up to and spoke to her, I said "hello you alright?", I made her laugh she made me laugh, as we were walking back up to our bungalow, it was mad because there was like all the disney charactersn just walking about meeting and greeting the kids and families, it was fantrastic, there was a person there holding a monkey, you could go up to and stroke it.

It was just so nice like such a nice place, when we got back to the bungalow we chucked on a bit of suntan lotion filled our water bottles up and got into the car and made our trip over to disney land, we had main parking which again was thanks to make a wish foundation, we went ot the car park parked up and went inside the park, we had a special card on us where we could first like get frist in line to all the rides on disney land, it was so magical to see the big disney castle, and to see al these people having a laugh and a joke, yeah it was actually fantastic, we went on to the rides and see more disneyu characters, the chipmunks, the soldiers out of toy story, we see loads of different goofys from different stories, in different outfits.

There was massive trailers and big lorrys going past, with casts of high school musical and as the vans would drive past they would all be singin and dancing, which was another great thing, I guess its all just entertainment that everyone loved, obviously I really loved it and I wish I could go back there as soon as I can, so afgter doing everything we did having a great day we was buying little memrobillia bits, key chainsd, tea cups etc, we were going to the resteraunts in there we were enjoying the amusments and the rides, the day come to an end and we jumped in the car and we was our way back when we noticed a few american shops we came across the supermarket out there which is called wal-mart, there was a shopping centre with many of shops in it, which wass filled with your sports shops, your fancy shops, your jewlerrs and all those sorts of things, we had the whole of the week to do that, so we didnt make any stops, what we did was make mental notes of where all the shops were so we could visit them during the week, which again was exciting, we went back to the give kids the world village, we had something to eat in the cafe which was totally free, then went to the ice cream parlour where I got a massive knicker blocker glory ice cream or something like that, it was a big ice cream in a massive glass cup with sprinkles and strawberry sauce on it, there was everything on it there was loads of strawberriees in it choclates everything, I didnt finsih I couldnt finish it luckily we were allowed to take our ice creams back to our bungalows, when I giot back to the bungalow I put mine in the freezer I had a shower and went to sleep, the next morning I completley forgot about it but we woke up done the same thing of going to the cafe having breakfast, I see that lovely again, we made eachother laugh it was great to see a smile on her face and see her excited to see me again, and talk to me, then we went to disney lands and orland studios, we went into a different park, which was orlando florida park, this was more rides then in disney land and it was only 2 seconds away we it was amazing went on all the rides, orlando florida was all the themes to all the films jaws, beetlejuice, spider man, harry potter and everything thats been made by universal, monsters inc etc. We went on all those rides we went in to a nice lunch area we then bought lots of memrobilia bits again which was fantastic, then obviously we wnet back to the bungalow, it was really amazing because we went back and when I went in to my bedroom the cleaners would go in there everyday and tidy and clean but when I would go back in there from whatever we did during the day there would be loads of gifts in my bedrooom like baseball cardss, to board games to teddys, drinking boittles, towels, t-shirts, loads of things its jus amazing to see, to see that its just fantastic and amazing and just a great feeling, when that happens, dvds, games and whatever, I just really loved it there it was such a fantastic place that you couldnt imagine anything like it, you would have to go there to see what its like to understand what I mean its just really really really fantastic, and thaty night we popped out to the theatre place where we watched a mickey mouse show, I actually, they ask people ot get up on stage or whatever so I got on stage and like as I doing what thewy were asking me to do like doing funny things and what not, I thought it was amazing, I looked up at one point and see loads of people with smiles on there faces, I don't know what it is but I just love to see people smile, seeing big grins on peoples faces and for them to look happy, so I did that got a few kisses off minnie mouse, shook mickey mouses hand, it was fantastic feeling I can't express how great it was, we then went back to the bungalow and I guess I just went to sleep and had a great time, the next morning came which was my birthday, during the night they put a letter through my letter box wehich said arnie when you wake up in the morning we want you to come straight to the reception and collect your gift which was so exciting so got dressed and went out, outrside the front door was a big helium baloon saying happy birthday, I went to the reception and they had this massive chest like a pirates treasure chest and they said you can have anything you want inside the box, dont get me wrong it was wonderful but it was mainly toys and dolls for the little ones, I loved it anyway, I see an ice hockey shirt and took that back home with I love all the american sports, that day I wore that very hockey shirt with a t-shirt under it, then went for a bit of breakfast and then began the day again we went down to where everything was the disney land the orlando studios, the next bit was like I can't remember the name I think it was adventure land or whatever, There was all rides and like big animals out in the jungle everywhere, lizards, spiders, insects and stuff like that which again obvioulsy was a brilliant day. We thoroughly enjoyed it, we went to this resteraunt in this advernture place whiuch was proppa done up like jurrasic park, there was loads of dinasaur models, we had a nice bit of munch and we carried on with our activities in the park, on the rides, exploring all the animals and creatures, it was just a great day.

As we were coming back in to the car park I noticed a resteraunt called the bubba gump shrimp which is off of forrest gump the film and I love that film so much and I reckon I watch it about 5 times a week I guess I could sit there and say every single word without fail where I have seen it so many times, I went into that shop and I was lookiong and it was just amazing to see the t-shirts and glasses with quotes and stuff from bubba gump and the film and I loved it, next thing was a shrimp resteraunt I didn't go in there though cos I don't like shrimp to be fair, but there was lots of other foods like mcdonalds and whatever, but I had to make sure I went into the shop and buy a couple of thingsa in there, I remember going into the super store walmart, for an essex boy living in england wal mart is an amazing place to go because I had never seen it before, it literally has everything you need from food to clothing to outdoor stuff to from everything, we went in there and got some american foods, there was this cereal called lucky charms we bought, we got some baby roof bars, coke, root beer and a few t-shirts of mickey mouse and whatever, we bought some big red chedwing gum which was cinnamon, my brother always bring us back some home when he goes to arizona, and we defiantly like it.

On that day as well we got back early from the theme park so it was quite early so we went and had a look in the mall cos it was my birthday I got treated my mum bought me a adidas tracksuit and a gym bag which I really liked, I got some money in my bday cards and stuff, I noticed there was some stalls in this mall that were selling these big cowboy belts and wallets. I really love the sport baseball, I've played it but I have never been to a game but i'm always reading up about it and looking at the hiostory of it I just love the game, so as we were walking out I noticed there was baseball jersey sho, we went in there, my mum was gonna buy me a jersey, but they didnt have any chicago cubs jerseys which I really love and follow, I just love the jerswey they had one I think but it was way too big of a size so we didn't get it, but my mum made me a promise that before we go home that I was gonna get one so I was really happy about that, we then went back to the village, I went to the basket ball hoops and was shooting some hoops, I then went back in and got in the shower, we then went out to the resteraunt area had something to eat then went to the theatre are to see what was going on, it was really exciting, I thought it was really good to do that for my 15th birthday, it was really really good, the next day which was the 2nd to last day I was standing there we went out and instead of going to the theme parks we went to the wild life place and that was all like every single animal like a zoo, still with mickey mouse and siney characters all dressed up in safari gear, which was amazing, to see the models they make of little things like wheel barrels, trucks, train rides we would go on and see al the animals like the lions in the woods, meerkats and waterfaklls with hippos and stuff. We had a bit of lunch there and spent the rest of the day there it was really exciting we ended up in a sea world I think, thats where the big whales were sharks, fish and c acouple of rides, we then sat down and watched the whale show, it was really amazing to see what the whales could do, just to see the differewnt sea animals, it was really good, that night we went to wal mart and bought some more goodies and treats dr.peppers and food, we then went back to the bungalow and had something to eat and was watching tv, and eating crisps and dip and chilling out it was just really nice, the next day we went to erm I think it was our last day, so we was just mooching about for the day, I remember we came across like these road side shops, like a road side sport shop, we went in there to see if they had that chicago cubs jersey but it was amazing to see american sports gear for sall and have there own big shop, obviously over hear its football rugby cricket and whatever, over in america its american football, baseball, hockey, ice skating its really good to see those sort of jerseys like a whole new experience for me, they had other stuff in there as well, like baseball shoes, baseball bat, american footballs and sportsweat, it was really good, but they didnt have the jersey I was looking for, it was the last day and I really wanted to get a jersey to take home, so I bought a new york yankees jersey which I do like very much. As soon as I bought it I put it on straight away, we was walking along these row of shops we went into a golf shops and it's just mad to see the people the way talk how friendlly they are, as were driving back we noticed there was a mini golf place, which we pulled up to had a couple of games of mini golf, it was like a night on an island, as there was a lake around the mini golf course which had all crocodiles in it actually, which was really good, there was waterfalls and it was really hot, I think cos we was on one hole I think it was the 16th hole and we had to go into like a cave under a waterfall, and I put my head and hat under the waterfall, and I took my hat off and put it under the waterfall but the weather was so hot it felt amazing, then I put my hat back on and I just felt nice and cool, it was just a fantastic day and a fantastic trip it was just amazing.

We went back to the village and started packing our stuff, we then went into the special c ave with the stars and stuff and they told me to put my star up and make a wish, so I did put my name on in and said my wish or a dream and they did all the magical fairy tale noises and I granted my wish I guess my stars on there ceilings till this day, i'd love to go back to see it now, I have a certificate saying that my star is the fourth one in from the fifth line back, so if I did ever go back I would know where it is, it was a fantastic experience so we left and took thed hire car back, we then got a lift to the airport, when we go checked in and that, then we was waiting for the plane, I had a couple of dollars on me and some change like cents or nickels whatever, and quarters, I just went to the little sweet tuck shop, I had big hand luggage so I filled it with all these american sweets which I brought back to england, then we got on the plane which was exciting, cos i'm not one to go on a plane every year but I was sad as well because we were leaving florida obviously, then we got on the plane got all settled in which was nice and exciting as well, then away we went and we flew back, this time I got to meet the captain of the plane my mum had mentioned to the cabin crew who I was and what I been through so the cabin crew took me up to the top tier cabin in the 1st class where the cock pit was I met the pilot shook his hand and spoke to him he was so friendly and the cabin crew new my past of my illness and they were just so friendly, it was such a great experience I would love to go back there anytime. It's just a great feeling when your flying back in to England and when the plane lands on the ground and you just feel ah im back home, but on the flight back I was pretty tired actually and I fell asleep about an hour left to arriving in london, when we had landed I was still asleep and really tired, at that point I was still a bit weak and ill, luckily I had bought my wheel chair I was getting wheeled through the airport still half asleep with a blanket on me and everything. We got all set and ready to leave with our bags and what not, then we was outside to the typical english weather where it was cold and rainy, we then got in a taxi and went home, we got home and it was nice cos my mates come round and see me, so I was telling them about what a lovely holiday it was and showing them pictures and everything, the fruits the sweets I managed to get out there that io brought home, and some of the presents I got from the village, my traksuit and baseball jersey just telling them about the experience then they left it was about 12 in the afternoon and me and my mum fell asleep must of been jet lagged I think we then didnt get wake back up until about 9 in the night, we woke up and we was like amazed as what the time was and it was quite dark outside so we had a bit of dineer then went back to sleep, but then it was a struggle to get bacxk to bed, where we slept for quite a whilst but then we finnally did fall asleep, then wokje up the next day, what a great experience it was going to the USA also the experience of going to disney land and meeting mickey mouse and all the othe r disney characters and it was huts an amazing experience, but now, to this day on I do regret loads of things because I chose to go on that holiday at the time which was only a couple of months after I finish my chemo and I was so much stronger from day 1 but I wasn't that much stronger but still not that strong, I think back now and think I wish I went maybe a few years after or later or even at this time, where I feel so much better in myself, where I am more fit, more engergetic, more stamina and I think it would of been a good time to do it now, at the time it was really hot and that did take it out of me, but of course I enjoyed it and do wish I could go back out there and there are some things I regret as I said that I love baseball I love all the american sports and whatever, and I never got the chance to go to a baseball game or go see a football game or basketball or whatever, there is something else I wanted to do cos obivously my brothers in the army and hes got loads of pictures of out there in his big uniform with his weapons and gear and I wish I went to the army place and mention my self and get a few pics with them and the american police, I would of love to of gone there and just got a few pictures with the swat team, standing behind me with there weapons and kit and even the experience of getting into a yellow cab or something like that, when I do go back those will defiantly be the things I will try to do, even as well just to go to mcdonalds and order a BIG BIG BIG Mac cos the mcdonalds in england have really small meals compare to the ones out in the US we did go to a mcdonalds in the airport in the US, cos we only got little meals, I would like to experience the big meals and see how much of it I can eat and whatever but I guess thats waiting for another day,

Chapter Six

BACK TO REALTY I GUESS

Continued with my normal life of getting better:

beening back in england back to the norm of everyday life schooling out with friends was oibviuously great I loved it I look forward to the training day with almunia sometime this year was exciting and I was just going day by day and taking it as it comes and goes, doing everything I do to help with my physical achievements by carrying on with gym and home workouts, thwere was this one time this year june I think it was actually tct rang me up and said they wanted to do another video of me and obviously I was so much healthier and I had hair put on weight and just looked also much better nand I was so positive in my mind, so I went to this video shooting, which was in the emirates at arsenal it was strange in a way cos it was empty, no one was there from arsenal, we got the car from where I lived and drove up to arsenal and had permission to park under ground the stadium at emirates, I met up with the ladies and the girls from TCT and they told us what was gonna happen and I generally thought it was me and a few others but it was just me and we went right up to the top tier, there I was sitting on one of the chairs on the stands and there was a person in front of me holding a big camera and I had to tell him stories of what was going on and how felt and what tct has done and helped me and what I thought of em, it was really good to just do it on my own, then we went back down to the actual field and then the camera crew explained they wanted a clip of me going through the tunnel with my head held high which I must say once again was a great experience, it was really good, the next week they rang me up and said have a look online at the TCT charity videos and I did there I was the way they did it was really good, cos when I did the Holly Willoboughy video I was really ill at the time I was bald I was skinny I had a feeding tube up my nose and this one I had done at emirates I had hair I had put on a bit more weight, I looked healthier its amazing how they put the videos together they put the video of me with Holly when I was talking then cut it and said 1 year on and put the video of me in the emirates stadium and the difference in me was truly amazing, I even sounded more positive I was which obviously made me feel good cos they wanted me to do the video to show how TCT have supported and helped me through and me motivating my self and being positive to helpo my self, by this time, arsenal were still the charity for TCT and I had been invited to many of the arsenal games cos arseanl give tct tickets and I was invited so many times to go see games, and I've now sat in every single row in the arsenal stadium. It's just fantastic, which is really good for me as im an arsenal supporter, Ive been on the pitch i've met the players had tours round the stadium and doing all that stuff was really fun, the end of the season came and me and my mate jack got asked to go nout on pitch and hold up some signs saying thank you when the stadium was full because I think every seat in the stands was filled with fans and we got to walk out on live TV with signs to say thank you for everything, that was reall exciting on the last game for arsenal on that season Arsenal played Liverpool, TCT asked me to go out on pitch on my own with Arsene Wenger and Roger Doultry the saint patron of TCT, and collect the cheque for how muhc Arsenal raised for TCT which was another great experience as well, where there was no empty seats and it was literally jam packed. So yeah I walked on to the pitch with Wenger and Roger Doultry and held up the Arsenal t-shirt and on the back it had up how much we had raised, obviously there was loads of pics taken and we was on sky sports this was all pre game, after that we went in to the boxlevel and stayed in there to watch the game, obviousuly I was with the girls from teenage cancer trust and roger doultry and there was another guy there called Geoff Thompson he is an Australian cricketer like one of the best, he said he was gonna send me a gift of a signed pic of him, we was watching the football having a good time, It was really nice, I would carry on with my normal day routine with days leading into weeks and weeks leading into months, just with I use to do, I guess it was a bit more exciting at school, I was a bit more stronger I could have more of a laugh with my mates, and join in with sports and carried on joining with football games not being as good as what use to be but still getting involved, my mates calmed down a bit and it was really good me and my mates would go out on to the playing field so it was better then sitting in side being out in the sun with everyone, yeah it was really good, I guess at the time I was still a bit weak not as strong but I did feel good in my self and I still wanted to do stuff that other people would of said no I cant do that yet cos im not strong enoguht or not well enoguh or whatever but I did start getting back into my sports, I was doing more physical stuff in school which knackered me out but I loved doing it, trhere was a sports day type of thing that the school did, we had various house colours like yellow, red, blue, green whatever which what the teams were, one of the sports days activity weas 5 a side football on the playing field and like I was in the red team and I wanted to be the goal keeper my mates were like are you sure and what not that day I went all out brought in my gloves boots shin pads got proppa kitted out, all the stuff i've sadly hadn to put away but then I thought nah i'll get it out and have a go see how I get on, we all went in the sports hall, got in our teams and it was all thew years together. I rememeber we were sitting in there and there was this year 8 boy who thought he was a cheeky chappy, thought he was a hard nut, he started laughing and taking the piss out of me, He said if your hand is bigger than your face then you have cancer, obviously at the time I didnt know it was a joke, so like a melon I put my hand to my face just because I didn't know the joke and he pushed my hand propa into my face, at the time I had no co-ordsination no balance, but I didnt like that so with my left arm I went to punch him, I had no co-ordination so obviously it werent hard but I still caught him in the face and I said don't ever take the mick out of me and dont make jokes about cancer because its not fair and it certainly isnt funny, from that day he realised that was bad and that made me mad to be fair, the team leader, captain of the red team, said year 11 red team lets get ready to start the football game so went out on the pithc started playing, we had to play every other coloured team on the pitch, at the end of the games, it was lunch I was sitting out on the playing field on the grass, they all said to me arn you was amazing you havent lost it, you still got the goalkeeping skills inside of you and you are slow but thats fair enough that gave me a real confidnce boost, it made me happy and proud of my self, it was an amazing feeling, I finally got my confidence back in school, I was more polite to teachers and more nice to students I felt as if I was more mature in myself due tpo what I had been through, so yeah I had more confidence, started to get back into being the class clown, no where as bad as what I was but still being a joker again, telling little jokes and making everyone laugh, I felt comfortable again, like everything was back to normal, I think school was a great time for me to spend time with my mates, playing football, having a laugh and seeing eachother every day, we then went into year 11 which was the last year, this is where a few priorties came, we had to pick our subjects we wanted to study in GCSE lessons in year 10, but year 11 is so much mor important cos your exams are almost near and you have to really start knuckling down, and getting mor education or whatever, praciticing exams, I guess though at the time I was not bothered, obvioulsy I missed my childhood at school, At the time I really wasnt bothered, When we was in lessons for our GCSE I wouldnt be interested, I would be acting up, joking and messing about. I was very laid back and just thankful for still being here today, I then took on a role as a prefect, we were role models for younger students, on our lunches and breakes we would stand in various school parts to monitor the hallways and corridoors, we was there to regualte rules and this was a big priortity and I wore the prefect badge and tie, It was laugh as my mates all became prefects we was picked various days to be on prefect duty monitoring hallways, which meant we had to give up our time. So we couldnt go out and play football and what not, I did my prefect duty with my good mates and it would be laugh we would eat our lunch in the corridors, in the end it would end up being a good time, they then made a tea room for all the prefects. They supplied us with tea and biscuits so when we didnt go out and play football we would go in there and chill and have a joke around still but have the privellege of our private room, don't get me wrong I did love to play football and what not but I was getting tired as well, so I would enjoy sitting and having a biscuit and tea. Which in one sense I kinda feel out of order on my mates because I would make them come and sit in with me, yeah there was the other prefects in the room but they were not as close as we were, so I would make my mates come in with me all the time which stopped them from playing football but they have always said to me where always here to look after and support you and they would love to give up there time just so I dont get bored so it was really good, I guess iot was a laugh as well we would have few jokes and just a right laugh, I guess schooling carried on as normal, in the mean time I was missing a lot of school time due to mri scans, blood tests, opticians etc, there was always days where I had to I think every week for a past year I think I missed about a year of schooling, so I missed a lot of lesson time, study time and whatever, so when the time came and I was ready for my gcses I wasnt that smart if you know what I mean, the lesson I took were, btec sport, science my english math and p.e, I passed my science and btec sport, but failed my english and maths, my english due to my spelling thats it, I didnt pass my maths obviously cos I was never really good at maths, due to, my p.e I didnt pass due to my physical ability. My btec sport was more written then physical, the year and 2 months I was in the hospital I was learning more about the body about how it works which gave me the knowledge I needed to pass my btec sport as it was about science and the body and sports, which was an advantage of being in hospital, also being heavily in to sport was an advantage, they were my two favourite lessons, which I did pass which made me feel really confident and good. Obviously due to the lack of schooliung obviously I was out I didnt pass my maths english and my main subjects really, but it didnt bother me at all as I like to say I am who I am im proud of who I am and what I have achieved, and I know obviously you need those skills in life but I feel as if i've got what I need to go on in life and to succeed in life and I feel good on my self then obviously school ended. And it was nice I've stayed close with all my mate some have drifted away, which I still talk to but I dont see as much, my best mates I see em all the time, there great lads, which is really nice, I started college to do a health and social course to pass that hopefully to help other cancer patients however I didnt pass it, the next year I did another course of health and social care, I then did an apprentice as health and social care in a old peoples home for about 4 months, but I felt really out of place maybve the old are not my scene, i'm determined to help young cancer patients I guess, that have still got the push inside of them to get on life, I mean I do respect the elders but I mean most of them in this care home and dementia, alczheimers, basically physically cant get on I felt as if I was wasting my time there so I give that up and stopped working there, I started mucking about doing stuff with my dad, hes a carpenter and has been for 45 years now so we do gardens, sheds, big cabins, log cabins, buildins, now he is semi retired, he just does little jobs of shed repairs and garden repairs, in the same boat its like rehab for me im picking up heavy objects, walking on uneven ground, painting sheds fences, pushing weel barrels using hammer and nails, its all therapy at times, there are times when it is very difficult but I never give in and I never get angry I just get even, I always think to myself right how am I gonna get passed this and I just think calm down and try and get it done, I love doing what I do.

I feel in myself that iom grown up inside I do feel as if that im an old man myself more mature I guess in some ways I've got more responsibility, instead of just mucking about, im in the gym everyday, im not one who goes out partying, clubbing, listening to all the up to date music I dont like alchohol im not a drinker, I dont like smoking, im more of the person to sit in doors and watch films with my mates, go out to eat, go out to nice places, drink teas, drink water, go on days out which I do really enjoy, but I guess everyone feels completeley different to everyone else, but that just me, it was bout 201 a bit of bad news my mum unfortunatlkey got diagnosed with breast cancer it distraughted her and I guess I motivated her and we helped eachother, my mum was there for me 24/7 every day every night, I helped her as well we would motivate eachtoher, she made the descision to amputate her breast and me mum was on the chemo for a few months, and she came off it, since then everythings been okay and till this day on shes improving evertyday dsue to my motivation with my mum obvioulsy I love my mum so much I can't express how much thankfullness and greatfulness I have for my mum I feel like its my turn to show it back to her and help her out, me mum was a heavy drinker of the old alchol sadly at one point it was to much stress maybe of the cancer the memories of me and many other stuff that was on her mind and one night she decided to take her own life she had an overdose of paracetamols whilst she was drinking alchol which obviously harmed but thanks to the angels, and god, and jesus christ that shes here today and recovering from an alcholic, its made my mum see a better light now shes more happy and positive, me and my mum do more together now and its like it takes the drink off her mind, so we go up the gym together and we er just spend more time together which is really nice, I do love my mum, shes a brilliant women, I just cant express how grateful I am for my mum, she is the number 1 girl in my eyes I would never let aything happen to her, she is just fanmtastic, I couldnt dream for any other mum, this is why this is book is for you mum, a year went by its now 2011 I finally feel strong enough and i've head that trainign day with almunia got a train up there then the transpoirt picked us from the station me and my mate chay maffia and took us to the arsenal trainign ground, where almunia was waiting for us, I didnt think we would actually have a trainging session so I had no kit on me what so ever, I had turned up in a nice pair of jeans shoes and shirt, Manuel said to me wears your gear and I went oh no I didnt expect to be kicking a football around so went into the changing rooms so luck enough I had the same size hand and boots as him, he gave me a spare kit, we went out on the pitch had a kick about, that was a really fantastic day, I was back in my glory days jumping about with my idol and my best mate Chay, I had them both taking shots at me, I did get worn out but I felt pleased worn out it was a great day and afternoon, we was training for about hour and ahalf had a shower got changed then went into the cafe area, it was literally only me my mate Chay and Almunia had a cuppa and a sandwich, as were walking out it was just mad like mad because I see another one of my idols david seamen he was my idol back in the day there he was he came walking in to the training ground I didn't know who he was at the start cos he has now cut his hair he has short hair now I was standing there looking at him, and I went omg your david seamen he went yeah thats it mate I am, so went up to him and got his signature, I had no paper on me or nothing all I had was tissue from mcdonalds I had earlier on, so anyway on this bit of tissue I've got him to write to arnie, best wishes david seamen, but yeah I've still got that in the loft in my treasure box which will never be opened, or given away. Off we went me and my mate chay got on the transport to the train station then our way home and that was just another amazing day.

I carried on with my day to day business obviously tryna get well with my rehab up the gym just doing what sports I could really, I started college I was doing a health and social course, theres 3 steps in it a level 1, 2 and 3 due to my school qualifications I thought I had to start at level1 I went to my college intervierw and done the test and whatever and I actually got into level 2 obviuously that was good cos that meant I didnt have to do the level 1 then go on to the level 2, I could do the level 2 then go straight on to my level 3, obviously I met new people who were lovely people which I had a laugh with, my mate from secondary school was in the same class as me doing the same course which was good having a familiar face to be with and meet new people with, it all went from there, I was doing my classes whatever, I guess because I missed my whole year 9 and part of my year 10 there the kind of years where you muck about ahave a laugh with your mates and what not so I guess I tried to re live those moments cos I was doing my work and stuff like that but I was talkling and mucking about and having a laugh more, there was all lovely pupils in there who new what I had been through which was really fantastic, my level 2 course lasted for whole year unfortunatley I didnt pass it, I was a couple of marks and I did it again this time obviously all my class mates had stepped up and were moving up a level to level 3 going to do apprentices etc, obvioously I had to stay in with the level2 and I dont think I liked so I didnt go on to it again, I didn't fancy doing it because I failed it the first time round. I had 4 weeks off doing nothing in that time I thought aboput it and I did wanna get back into the health and social care, so I thought I would take out a health and social care apprentichship. So I went back to the college and told them what I wanmted to do, I remember going in to the office and even the teachers theres was about 4 teachers in there at a time, you got your sociology teachers your mental sociaology tecahers, you got your social workers in there and your english teachers etc. all of them were amazed as to my reasons behind what I wanted to do and my reason behind the career I chose, they have never had anyone in that college that has done it for the same reason, they say every pupil that wants to do that course is because of they have no ambition they just wanna work in a care home or just do it to earn some money do you know what I mean? So obviously I said I wanna be a social worker for patients who have had cancer to motivate them and there families and they were so amazed with my positive attitude towards life which was the apprenticeship, I started my apprentice in vange, essex I was there for about 4 weeks, I didnt like it I was dreading going I just didnt like it it just wasnt me I just did like doing it or whatever, maybe the reason was cos they were old people that had physical disabling illness' and they couldnt do alot but they didnt wanna do alot of things cos they just wanted to sleep and rest or whatever, they had me as activities co-ordinator, that was good in one sense so I didnt have to do the nitty gritty stuff like cleanign etc. so I was getting everyone up tryna get them to do stuff but that was good gfor me I like getting people motivated, as io said theyre old theyre ill and alot of the didnt wanna do anything, that kind of in one sense wound me up, as im the type of person who wants to get people up and going moving and get people going, obviuosly they didnt want to, I quit that and stopped working for them, I felt I was wasting my time nothing was happening and that was the end of that, I quit that course, and gave it another 6 weeks rest, I did not wanna get back into school all the writing and what have ya, I didnt wanna do the apprenticeship cos it was only care homes so I thought I dont wanna do it, what grinds my gears is that you see social workers who go into hospitals and talk to cancer patients like young children, adults, teens, and they all sit there with there legs crossed writing on a piece of paper and it doesnt seem as if there listening I remeber once when I had a social worker I didn't have to I didnt want to really and I only spoke to her the once, she was in the ward and came to talk to me, at the time I motivated the worker more than they did me, I remember sitting there and she said to me oh I know how you feel, and whatever and I stopped and thought no you dont know what I feel cos you dont know what i've felt the pain I went through the damage thats been done to my body, my balance, eyes etc, which probably gave me spur on to be a social worker, what grinds my gears is that somebody train to be a social worker doing 8 yerars in school then going into hospitals talking to people when they havent got a cluew what that patient feels like, do you what I mean? Then someone like me who cant get the grades and pass the courses, to become a social worker, I know more then that person whos been trained for however long, anyways I stiopped on the education route, and went back to working with my dad, doing bits here and there, I really wanna start my own charity and call it the proud face of cancer, in which I can offer my own help to patients that have had cacner and familys that have had cancer sufferers it was only a charity where I could offer patients to come to pizza hut or down the harvester or whatever to talk about there feelings and experiences, dont gfet me wrong I do get some people speak which is really good but I havent got loads of people to organiuse I charity to take people out in groups and whatever so that didnt go very well, I started getting more in contact with TCT and teens unite to see if they could help in any sort of way, but the thing is im down in the south east of england and teens unit and TCT are a right trek away from me, so its hard for me to get to and from a job, so there was no lead into that, so it kind of stopped, I was just working with my dad and one day I thought about writing a book, so here I am writing this book, the way I look at it is if I can't great the grades to talk to people in hospitals then I can send my book in and have people look on to it as motivations, to see what I've been through and for people to have the same attitude as me and come out fighting, so I went on year by year as what I always do going out with my mates popping down the snooker hall, going david lloyd with my dad doing minor exercises, in the gym swimming, luxury jacuzzis and the spa area, it was really good, I even started to do some ballet me and my dad went to barleylands and noticed there was a ballet school there for my balance and posture because it still wasnt 100% correct it was on every Wednesday so on a Wednesday I would go down there and get in my ballet outfit, it was nothing like the swan lake just a few stretches and balances, I was doing really well it was really good, the teacher even said if I do another 2 or 3 lessons like this I could be moved in to the group which made me feel good, but in dunno in my self I felt a bit not nervous but I didn't wanna go in as the group had no balance problems and they could do it perfectly, I didn't wanna go in there and ruin a play or anything like that and even my self which was like simple stuff like standing on your toes and keeping your feet on the floor and swiping it and stepping forward, it was hard for me so I used to get frustrated all the time, I think since I've had the cance I've grown up And matured so much in my self im only 19 years of age but all my friends call me grandad arn, which I dont mind I like it really I guess since day 1 I've always loved 60s music, since I got the cancer I dont like todays music, or house drum n bass, I hate strobe lights and all that bumping and grinding im not the type of person to go our clubbing and boozing or whatever, im more the type of person to go out for a meal at a resteraunt come home watch a film and chill out really and I care about everyone I ring my mates all the time make sure there okay, my 17th birthday my 18th and my 19th all at home big bbqs with all my friends, I do have quite a few people and every year every birthday its been the same friends and more, I really do like it my mates love come round as wel as they never really get to see me coming out and drinking, its nice the amount of times theyve said to me when the old birthday cake comes out they go to me speach speach speach and I do say a speach, and the speach I say all the time is thank the lord for my friends and family, I find that really lovely, its surprising the amount of people who have stuck by me me my main matês Chay maffia, tom archer, tom ryan, tom oconnel, bayden brown, tarsi tigere and many of the guys theyve always stuck by me and theyre my close mates as I say I have millions of friends but I only have a few mates its very very hard in this day and age to have loads of mates, who acxtually care and stick beside you and do worry about you, as one of my friends tom ryan he only lives up the road from me hes a keen sports man I've played football with him many of times, played against eachother on different teams, this was before I was unwell, we was playuing against eachother we was drawing it was 0-0 coming to the end of the game tommys team had a corner kick obviously I was keeper at the front post ready to save the ball, now my mate tom at the time was about 3 foot tall, hes an irish boy and hes really small so he was at the back post and the ball come flying over me and ol tommy there headered the ball into the goal so theres my mate just scored against me, we still keep in contact from school as I said he only lives up the road, I wasn't well enough to get back in to 11 a-side so we searched about and he found a 5 a-side football comp which was at the local community centre in Basildon, we got a team of us and started to play, which in one sense was really good I mean it was actually funny, I mean I used to love it I really enjoyed it, there was times when I let goals in or whatever but all my mates were so competitive when they lost they used to get really angry and upset, I was juist cool as a cucumber though I would just be happy to be stand there and play the game and at the end of the game I would bve the only one to go to the other team and congratulate there win. As my team would sit at the goal line with ump cos theyve lost, not upset with me just cos they've lost, that was just great to get back into fgootball, there was one time when we started playuing the 5 a-side football we turned up on the Friday which was under 30s, so it was me and my other mates and it was bunch of 30 year olds on the other side of the pitch I mean we lost that game I think we lost by like 9 – 5 but some saves I made were even congratulated by the ref and my mates, telling me cor arn you aint lost it, and stuff like that, I dont know wheteher it was a spur of the moment and I would just dive and get lucky, I would never mention my illness in the game or at all by this time I looked perfectly well, so they had no clue, proudest moment of that was defiantly the saves I had made It made me feel really proud of my self and ididn enjoy that, so I would carry on doing all of that going gym, ballet, my day to day life I wouldnt ever let anything get me down, whatever life had to throw at me I would just put it in the net and get on with it, I would do things day by day, theres even been times where I've been with my dad and if anything happened such as me falling over or whatyever, my dad would be like whats a matter with ya get up etc. Which I liked the humor of.

This one time we was all sitting down me my brother and dad having a cup of tea on a plastic garden chair and I fell off the chair backwards, and they both just looked at me like whats wrong get up then, it was so funny, we was all laughing our heads off, they didnt help me I just got up and was like who wants another cup of tea then. They didnt jump up and run to help me or nothing they just left me to get up and get on with it. I thought it was fantastic, like they'll be even times when me and my dad will be on a job and there would be un-even ground or whatever, I was screwing in a screw with my left hand and my dad was watching over my shoulder going to me how long you gonna take with that then, which made me laugh.

Thats part of life you can either make a joke out of it or sit there and cry about it. So thats what we did. I remember this one time a couple months into being diagnosed my brother chris had made us all sandwiches, he sat there infront of me and forced me to eat the sandwich, it was a corned beef and tomato sandwich was really nice. After my chemo and everything it didnt finish there, theres still regular check ups and exams, there was this one time I had foot drop due to the chemo I had an appointment with an orthopedic which was in stan more and they send I had to have a tenden transfer, so I went trhough that, I then had the operation I think it was about 2 hours long they said to me you wont be able to put weight on your foot for 6 weeks, but me being me asked for a pair of crutches cos there was no way I was gonna not move for 6 weeks, so I tried out the crutches but where I have no co ordination in my left hand my left crutched went all wobbly and almost fell over, there was no chance of me using the crutches to get about so I got a zimmerframe, the doctors had a good ol' crack about that, but the zimmer frame worked and I was fine with it I thought it was beautiful mate, but at times when I didnt wanna use it like walking to the kitchen and going to the toilet I would just walk on my leg knowing I shouldnt of, I was off work for 6 weeks, which was really annoying because I had been in hospital all that time then couldnt leave the house as well so it was a struggle even getting in the bath, especially after having my pic line in my arm and not being able to get it wet in the bath and whatever now I have to keep my leg out the bath and not get that wet cos of the cast, so the 6 weeks went past and I had to go to stanmore to get the cast off, I felt my big toe and ankle moving but they were still flopping so they booked me and appointment for 2 weeks time to check up, it didn't seem as if anything had changed, so when we went back they said my tenden could of been pulled up by another 2cm but they held off the operation till february so I could enjoy my christmas as it was november time by now, when february camer we had the operation so they put the cast back on and they said dont walk on it at all so I had to use my wheel chair, it was hard work walking on the zimmerframe as its alot of stress on my shoulders etc, so I had to use my wheel chair. I thought to myself I cant just sit in doors all day and do nothing, so I would go out with my mum shopping and out with her on her trips, it never stopped me going to the gym though, I would still take my wheel chair into the gym and be working my upper body strength and even work my left leg, alot of people who would see me would say wow what an inspiration as I never complained or give in,

I was so determined to get better and thats what I did. My dad come up with the idea of me putting cling film round me like my feeding tube and picc line so I could go swimming, where as most people would be to scared, so instead of letting your muscles just staying out of use you cant be scared you have to go out there and try these things out dont be afraid of infections etc. I believe swimming is defiantly the best remedy for the body it takes away those aches and pains, I love the gym I go in the gym and just do those small weights justy to get my body and muscles working. It spurs you on to do that little bit more, it makes you feeli im n ever gonna give up and I think thats the attitude everyone should have, so I had the cast taken off from stanmore hospital but again I still dint feel as iof it was moving properly so there was an option of them fusing my ankle and toe, but I didnt want that done I dint like the sound of it, I felt like I had enough of all operations and everythhing so I've let it be, but to this day its not right but its so much better, I cant stand about and just worry about it cos it'll just get me more down, you have to think of yourself as lucky you see, its lucky you can do whatv you can do, Its lucky your not in hospital not able to move! Its those moments in the hospital that you feel grateful for what you have now, npot alot of people are not greatfull for what they have. Theres times I drive past the hospital and thank god that im not in there and thank for me being in a car or van or whatever with sun in my face. Theres always something you can think positive about, lets say youve lost a limb but you still have your mind you heart and you must still have the will to live.

Today was a sad day unfortunatley my mate Chris Rayner passed on, today is the day of his funeral, I mean many of my friends have passed on, from the cancer trust but I guess I was too young to go to there funerals so I've never been to a funeral in my life so today was the first time. And I woke up this morning and I had butterflies and I felt sick I've never been to a funeral so I didnt know what it was gonnna be like, I ended up getting dressed and getting ready for it on our weay down there as we was getting closer iwas getting butterflies the closer we got the more sick I felt, and sad, we got into the church and there was all the music flowers and candles and loads of sad people I guess about 10 mins went by then the boys brought in ol chrissy, I guess it was a shockl to actually see it in real life one of my mates in a box gone passed never to be seen again, it was sad on top of his box was his dirtbike helmet he used to love dirtbikes, rebecca said a few words about chris and hes achiewvements and the moneys his raised for charitys I guess itsa all over for chris, seeing him get taken out into the grave yeard and then put in the ground brought it all back to me really it was really sad I guess the way I look at it is everyone has there time and that day was chris' time and he went and I probably wont speak to him ever agin I do believe in angels and god and spirits, I do believe I will see his spririt again, and the human body dies and the spirit lives on, and I know I will see him again, whether it will be as im falling asleep in the shopping mall but I know ill be seeing him again im distraught hes a great mate and he'll never be forgotten in my eyes and im writing this book for you mate, We never see eachother daily but he was always in my mind. I just wanna say rip mate never forgotten you will always be there in my heart god bless.

Chapter Seven

MY PHOTOS THOUGH LIFE

Buster My 1st Dog

Me and my friends

Me and my Sister

Me and my Mum

Early school sports team
I was captain of the cross country
No1 Goal keeper for the football team
And because i was fast i played wing for
rugby team

Football team

Rugby team

Cross country running team

My Family

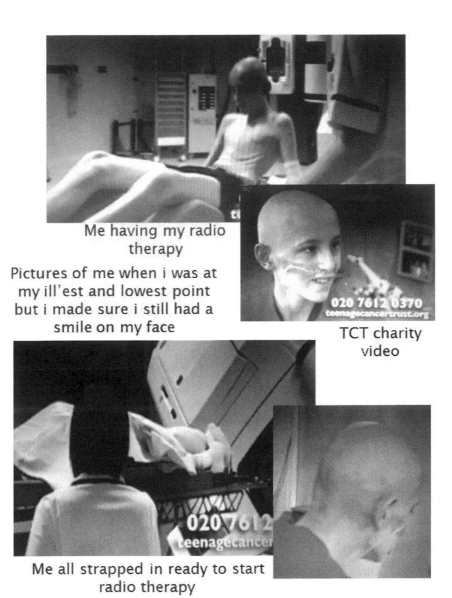

Me having my radio therapy

Pictures of me when i was at my ill'est and lowest point but i made sure i still had a smile on my face

TCT charity video

Me all strapped in ready to start radio therapy

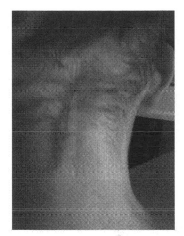

My scar on back of
my head and my
hair will never grow
back properly

A radio therapy mask it is
not mine because i crushed
mine because i hated it
but this is what they look

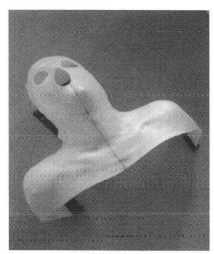

When i
had
double
vision

Meet holly on TCT
charity video

Home nurse got
glove caught during
cleaning my pic line

My head teacher got me free tickets for
the England game at the new Wembley
stadium

Charlie Flanerry me Chay Maffia
Josh Dean Tom O'Connell

Charlie me and
josh

When Theo came to T12

Me and my brother at Arsenal Emirates Stadium.

First game at England New Wembley.

Me and Holly. My bro really wanted to meet her, He has a massive crush on her! However he had to go back to work that day. It says "eat your heart out bill"

Wet flannel on my head. My home remedy cure for headaches.

Christmas 2008, Met the Arsenal team. Me with Emmanuel Adebayor.

Christmas 2008, Me and couple of guys on the TCT ward with Robin Van Persie.

Meet Theo Walcott during a Blood Transfusion.

Christmas 2008. Me and Robin Van Persie.

Best Birthday
Surprise Birthday
Present Ever. My
16th Birthday in
Hospital. Visit
from Manuel
Almunia!

Me and Theo
Walcott on T12

Me Manuel and jack
Chester TCT charity
day

Me van pirsie and
T12 guys

Me sagna and jack
Chester TCT
charity day

Teenage Cancer trust patron Roger Daltrey and
Arsene Wenger

Arnie Higgs is presented with an Arsenal shirt signed by goalkeeper Manuel Almunia

Arnie's back...getting fit after cancer fight local news paper pictures "Echo news, Basildon

Arnie Higgs with Teenage Cancer Trust patron Roger Daltrey and Arsene Wenger

Me and my dad continue my fitness regime after battling cancer

Florida
2K10

Castel of miracles

Ginger bread
house restaurant

My
special
star

Surf shack

The villa i stayed in

2010 Teenage
Cancer Trust
charity photo
shoot
" Hear wig go"

Me my bro and mum
x

Me my bro Suzanne
and mum x

Me my bro and Suzanne

Me bill and the
best man

Me my bro
and mum x

Brother bills
wedding 2011

Brother bill

Me the best man my brother
and second best man

Lads night out night
before wedding

Me and mum in
hotel pool

Mum brother and
suzanne

Me wearing my brothers
AAC Berea

Me and Tommy
Archer.

Me and Chay
Maffia.

Me and Lewis
Sciota

Me and Tommy
Archer.

Me and Kell

Me Chay Maffia & Tommy Archer.

Lewis Sciota, Bayden
Klingelstein, Me,
Harry Edgar

Me and Lilly
Harvey

Tom Archer, Harry Edgar, chay
Maffia, Bayden Klingelstein,
Jamie Jenkins and Me.

Me and Tommy Archer.

Me and Lewis Sciota

Me and Tommy Ryan.

Me and Lewis Sciota

Charlie Flannery, Bayden
Klingelstein, Robert Smith,
Harry Edgar, Arnie Higgs.

Stevie Smith and Me

Chay Maffia, Tommy Ryan,
Tommy Archer, Me, Lewis
Sciota.

Me and Tommy Ryan

Lewis Sciota me
Tommy archer and
Tom O'Connell.

Me and Tommy Ryan.

Charlie Flannery, Josh
Dean and Arnie Higgs

Harry Edgar, Tommy
Archer, Me, Lewis Sciota,
Bayden Brown and Josh
Dean.

Me, Tommy
Ryan and Lewis
Sciota.

Arnie Higgs,
Tarsi Tigere
and Kerri

Me with the guys.

Tommy Ryan, Lauren
Stevenson and Me.

Me with the guys at college.

Tommy Archer, Tommy Ryan
and Me.

Natasha Magnus, Sam Cross,
Emily Pryor, Lewis Sciota and
Me.

Lewis Sciota, Tommy Archer and Me.

Me, Lewis and the girls.

Me and the boys.

Me and Harry Edgar.

Me and everyone at a fancy dress party.

Me and Tommy
Archer.

Me and Sibel Aslim.

Me and the
guys

Me and Lily Harvey

Me and Siobhan

Amy, Natasha and
Me.

May 2014
Youth Cancer
Trust Holiday

2013 Sailing for the Ellen Macarthur cancer trust

Me and Lewis Sciota.
Prom 2011

Me and Katie Koutsombi.
Prom 2011.

Me and Katie
Prom 2011.

Me and Shannon
Prom 2011.

Me and Tommy
Archer. Prom
2011

Me and Sibel Aslim
2011 prom

Me tom O'Connell
rob smith 2011
prom

Me and Lauren
Slaughter 2011 prom

The
cufflinks
i wore
to prom
2011

Me and Kerry walker
2011 prom

October
2014 Youth
Cancer Trust
Holiday

MY RECOVERY NO PAIN NO GAIN

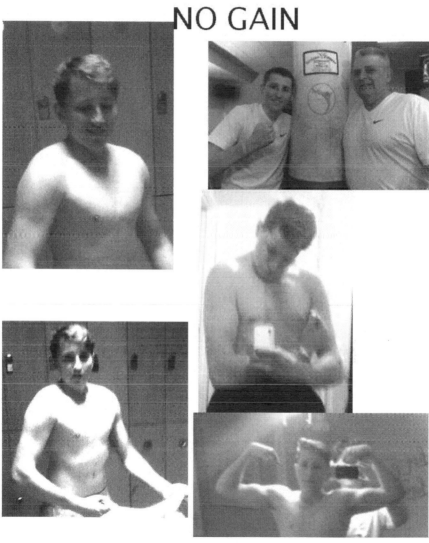

MY RECOVERY
Never Give Up

Printed in Great Britain
by Amazon